Praise for
A Taxonomy and Metaphysics of Mind-Uploading

"Starting with a very useful description of the ways that minds may be uploaded in the future, this book steps through some of the key philosophical
issues that mind uploading poses. What is consciousness? Is there personal
identity? What would the relationship of an organic person be to his mind
clone? If we can copy minds would that mean there is no free will? This book
makes a useful contribution to a debate that our children will undoubtedly
have a stake in."

—JAMES J. HUGHES PH.D. • *Executive Director, Institute for Ethics
and Emerging Technologies* • *Author, Citizen Cyborg: Why Democratic
Societies Must Respond to the Redesigned Human of the Future*

"Along with AGI, life extension and cyborgs, mind uploading is going to be
one of the major transformative technologies in the next century. Keith Wiley
has done us all a favor by providing the most careful conceptual analysis of
mind uploading that I've seen. The book is bound to become the standard reference regarding the various types of possible mind uploading, and the philosophical and scientific issues involved with each. As mind uploading moves
closer to reality, his analysis and others inspired by it will provide valuable
practical guidance to scientists and engineers working on the technology, as
well as ordinary people making decisions about their own potential uploading
to alternate physical substrates."

—BEN GOERTZEL PH.D. • *CEO of Novamente* • *Vice Chair at Humani-
ty+ Magazine* • *Chief Scientist at Aidyia Holdings* • *Advisor to the
Singularity Institute*

"Keith Wiley artfully blends key concepts, philosophy, and nascent technologies together in a fascinating work on mind uploading. His coverage of the
field is broad and deep, and jolts readers to see that a spark at the end of the
tunnel can now be seen in moving this technology from science fiction to science reality."

—ERIC KLIEN • *President of the Lifeboat Foundation*

"Keith Wiley has been involved with the pursuit of technology to accomplish
mind uploading or whole brain emulation almost since the very moment those
ideas crystalized and the terminology was born. In this book, he has diligently
applied that long experience and his attention to detail. Carefully separating
and describing the different paths and possible issues on the way to mind uploading, Wiley anchors the science and its philosophy. If you have ever been
confused by the cornucopia of concepts bandied about, or if you want to dig
deeply into the possibilities and consequences of mind uploading, then this
book is for you."

—RANDAL A. KOENE PH.D. • *Founder & CEO of Carboncopies.org* •
Founder of Minduploading.org • *Science Director for the 2045 Initiative*
• *Co-founder of the Neural Engineering Corporation* • *past Director of
the Department of Neuroengineering at Tecnalia*

A Taxonomy and Metaphysics
of Mind-Uploading

A Taxonomy and Metaphysics of Mind-Uploading

Keith Wiley

Humanity+ Press and Alautun Press

Published by:

Humanity+ Press and Alautun Press

http://humanityplus.org/projects/press

http://alautunpress.com

contact@alautunpress.com

Seattle, WA, USA

A Taxonomy and Metaphysics of Mind-Uploading

Keith Wiley

First edition 2014

Cover design by Keith Wiley

All illustrations by Keith Wiley

Photograph of Gorgonocephalus eucnemis

Public domain: Alaska Fisheries Science Center, NOAA Fisheries

http://www.afsc.noaa.gov/RACE/media/photo_gallery/photos/BrittleStars/gorgeucnemis.jpg

Video frame of katydid

Used with permission: Zain Sadi. Viral Spiral Group, Alex O'Brien (licensing executive)

https://www.youtube.com/watch?v=ZbIHK28Zl0M

ISBN 978-0-692-27984-7

Library of Congress Control Number: 2014915171

Contents

Figures   iii

Tables   iii

Preface   v

• *Section 1* •

1. **Introduction**   3
2. **Glossary**   13
3. **Taxonomy of Mind-Uploading Scenarios**   31
         Index   33
         Detail   35

• *Section 2* •

4. **Metaphysics**   65
         Motive   65
         Disclaimer (about language)   67
         Metaphysics   68
             Universals, Realism, Tokens, Occurrences   68
             Numerals   73
             Information, Matter, Energy, Entropy   76
             Relationship Between Tokens and Abstract Occurrences   78
         Type/Token Ambiguity   80
         Supervenience   84
5. **Minds**   89
         From Metaphysics to Minds   89
             The White Room   92
         Splitting a Mind   94
             Brains, Brain-States, Minds, Mind-States   94
             Realism of Numerals   100
         The Library of Anaxagoras   101
             Transformations   104

6. Debating Dualism and Considering Consciousness   **111**

    Dualism   111

    Consciousness   114

       Three Bugs   116

       Emergence   121

       Zombies   126

       Conclusion   128

7. Equality of Post-Upload-Procedure Minds   **129**

8. Free-Will and the Temporal Anthropic Principle   **135**

    Existentialism   138

    Conclusion   142

• *Section 3* •

9. Interpretation of Some Scenarios   **147**

     §1.1.1.1 In-place destructive conscious nanobot replacement   147

     §1.1.2.1 In-place nondestructive conscious nanobot brain-doubling   148

     §1.1.2.1.1 Brain-doubling with temporary biological shutdown   149

     §2.1.1 Frozen destructive scan-and-copy   152

     §2.1.2.1 Frozen nondestructive scan-and-copy: Natural environments   155

     §2.1.2.2 Frozen nondestructive scan-and-copy: Identical environments   157

     §2.1.2.3 Frozen nondestructive scan-and-copy: The White Room   158

     §2.2.1.1 Conscious destructive scan-and-copy: Teleportation   159

     §2.2.2.1 Conscious nondestructive scan-and-copy   159

     §3. Brain division   160

10. Conclusion   **163**

    Bibliography   **165**

    Index   **169**

Figures

1. Gorgonocephalus eucnemis (basket star)   49
2. Brain categories   53
3. Brain division   61
4. Platonic vs. Aristotelian type invocation   70
5. A sample of '5'-numeral-type tokens   74
6. Type/token ambiguity   80
7. Pattern identity of chess positions   91
8. Relationships of brain & mind metaphysical entities   99
9. Mind-state space (The Library of Anaxagoras)   103
10. Brain-state and mind-state transformations   107
11. Computer simulation of an ant mill   118
12. Katydid with confused sense of locomotion   119

Tables

1. Grouping of brain classifications based on functional
   abstraction of substrate   20
2. Mapping between metaphysical brain and mind   98
3. Spatio-temporal aspects of brain and mind   98

Preface

I can pinpoint my discovery of mind-uploading to a specific event, the purchase of *Beyond Humanity: Cyberevolution and Future Minds* by Gregory Paul and Earl Cox in 1997 [36]. I even remember precisely where I found it (in the vendor section at the International Conference on Genetic Algorithms). Even though the basic idea of transferring minds to computers significantly pre-dates that particular book, and even though I myself had certainly been exposed to the idea before, such as through science fiction examples, it was not until I read Paul and Cox's book that the full implications of the concept really clicked for me.

I soon discovered *The Mind-Uploading Research Group*, an online mailing list dating to the mid-nineties that discussed and considered mind-uploading from a variety of angles. Notable members included Joe Strout, who founded and organized the group, and Randal Koene, whose own career would subsequently tackle related topics head-on even as my path veered elsewhere.

In graduate school, I did not run straight at mind-uploading, but rather pursued artificial life, evolutionary algorithms, and image processing (of course my eventual dissertation was on none of those topics!). My subsequent forays into the work sector have similarly skirted mind-uploading as I have focused on massively distributed computing to keep the roof overhead. While high-performance computing is certainly important to modern neuroscience and other endeavors related to mind-uploading, I admit that I rarely find myself waist deep in the esoterica that mind-uploading research would entail. Nevertheless, I have remained committed to the idea, to the field, such as it is, and have followed its evolution and the community that has gravitated to it. At the same time, mind-uploading has matured, gaining greater recognition and perhaps shedding some of its giggle factor. MURG first transformed into the autologically-named *Minduploading.org* and then again into *Carboncopies.org,* which is currently an active online community. Both of these latter projects were spear-headed by the same Randal Koene, mentioned above, from the original MURG. Even the name of the field has evolved, spawning *Substrate Independent Minds* and *Whole Brain Emulation,* each involving related, but not identical, issues to mind-uploading.

As I have watched the field gain both popular awareness and underlying sophistication, all from my perspective as an early, if noncentral, enthusiast, I have amassed the following experiences: first, a broad familiarity with the expansive range of hypothetical mind-uploading scenarios that have emerged through both science fiction and philosophical debate; second, a corpus of such debates on the topic, both technically and philosophically, such that I am relatively well versed in the popular arguments and the common progressions of such debates; and third, the development and refinement of my own personal philosophy of mind and mind-uploading.

My experiences with mind-uploading have spawned a range of article-length pieces [51, 52, 53], but my recent writing quickly grew to a book-length project and ultimately became the work you are now reading. It is my hope that the reader finds elements of this book, either the taxonomy or the philosophical presentation that follows it, useful toward the development of his or her own philosophy of both mind and mind-uploading.

Acknowledgements

Randal Koene and Ben Goertzel are as knowledgable and experienced in this field as any current professional can hope to be. I greatly benefited from their feedback as well as their help determining publication options. My wife, Angeline Madrid, and my dad, R. Haven Wiley, in addition to Angela Consani and Lindsay Morahn, all provided invaluable editing, both copy-level and content-level. The forum members of Carboncopies.org, led by Randal Koene, and Penny University, initiated by Hoyle Anderson (a friend from as far back as natural memories can accommodate), were of great assistance. The discussions in those forums are often on the topics covered in this book and were of tremendous value in clarifying my exposition. I should also acknowledge reddit, in so far as the debates I found myself ensnared in there represented a sounding board, of sorts, against which I iteratively honed the description of my ideas. I would like to further thank my dad in particular for contributing to the hallowed tradition of philosophical engagement over several of the issues this book covers. Such discussions are crucial to the refinement and clarification of work of this nature.

About the Author

Keith Wiley has a Ph.D. in Computer Science from the University of New Mexico and was one of the original members of MURG, the *Mind Uploading Research Group*, an online community dating to the mid-90s that discussed issues of consciousness with an aim toward mind-uploading. He has written multiple book chapters, peer-reviewed journal articles, and magazine articles, in addition to several essays on a broad array of topics, available on his website at http://keithwiley.com. This is his first nonfiction book (aside from his dissertation). He currently resides in Seattle, WA.

Luminous beings are we, not this crude matter.

—Yoda

Section 1

$\sim 1 \sim$

Introduction

This book presents one possible metaphysical theory of mind with an emphasis on its implications for the audacious topic of mind-uploading, wherein a mind is *transferred* to another substrate, notionally some sort of computer. Specifically, this book addresses what I call *The Uploading Question*:

> **The Uploading Question**: *Under what circumstances, if any, and according to what interpretations, if any, might we judge a mind-uploading scenario to have successfully transferred a mind from one brain[1] to another?*

I must immediately take issue with the wording of the uploading question, even though it is my own conception. The problem is that our conventional vocabulary on these topics, and our assumptions about the feasible properties of, and transformations on, minds, are at odds with the theory and perspective presented in this book. The part of the question that rubs me the wrong way is the word *transfer*. There is no quick fix. Replacing it with alternatives, such as *copy*, *duplicate*, or *move* are all equally problematic. This book will eventually present a precisely defined alternative, which I summarize with the single term *split*,

---

[1] Throughout this book I will use a vocabulary that may differ slightly from common usage. Where my preferred vocabulary departs from convention, it is clarified in the included glossary. In this case, I am using the word *brain* to indicate any of a variety of concepts, as described in the glossary under *brain* and *substrate*, and in figure 2.

but in that short word is encompassed a thorough metaphysical model with which the reader is not yet familiar, and therefore I cannot use that word in the original statement of the question; I am forced to use our colloquial terminology, and *transfer* is as good a word as any other in such cavalier applications.

Much of this book serves the primary purpose of explaining and defending my offered views, with the remainder of the book applying those views to various mind-uploading scenarios to show one possible interpretation of those scenarios. By the end, the reader should comprehend how I view brains, minds, and mind-uploading, even if he or she ultimately disagrees with me. Note the precision with which I chose the title, namely the first word, "a" instead of "the". I do not claim to offer *the* definitive—much less authoritative—metaphysics of mind-uploading. Rather, I offer one such metaphysical model. This point is important because people tend to hold a variety of disparate and incompatible perspectives on these issues, and we are still at a sufficiently nascent stage of philosophical, psychological, and neurological investigation that we should leave all options on the table. That said, I believe the model I offer is amongst the more consistent, least prone to bias, and more precisely and thoroughly described.

I begin with a collection (organized as a taxonomy) of thought experiments as a basis from which any reader may develop his or her own philosophy of both mind and mind-uploading. I then offer my own metaphysical and philosophical positions. I would love to launch directly into the discussion, and it might seem straightforward to approach the topic. Given a definition for mind-uploading as *transferring a person's mind to a computer*, which is immediately comprehensible on a certain Hollywood level of sophistication, I could describe some common mind-uploading scenarios that have arisen both in the science fiction canon and in speculative futurist writing and ensuing discussions and debate, and then state the more popular objections to mind-uploading plausibility, even in theory. I could wrap up with an overview of my own theory and show why mind-uploading should be feasible under certain interpretations. It shouldn't take more than a brief essay to wrap that up.

However, I have participated in discussions on this topic enough times to realize that seemingly clear concepts get muddled on the battlegrounds of debate, with people ultimately talking around each other. Such discussions descend into cyclic arguments and often wander in focus, initiating with the main topic (can we transfer minds to computers?), only to discover that the participants don't agree on (or even understand one another's) conceptualizations of the issue, and then backtracking to clarify those foundational issues as a redirected topic of debate. In my opinion, such meandering accomplishes very little. Therefore, I prefer to start from more rudimentary philosophical principles and steadily work up to full-blown mind-uploading.

I have no illusions that after reading this book all readers will resoundingly agree with me. However, the organization I have chosen, if perhaps somewhat belabored, should minimize my two greatest concerns with respect to a more direct approach: one, that readers fail to thoroughly understand my argument, and two, that readers ultimately disagree with me even after my complete exposition. Surely, many will disagree, but the approach I have employed should mitigate final disagreement, and when it does occur, should further mitigate the risk that such disagreement stems not from genuine philosophical differences, but rather from a mere failure to comprehend my argument in the first place, i.e., a failure to communicate.

So, I beg the reader's patience.

When reading a book of this speculative nature, it helps to suspend disbelief with regard to the technological means to mind-uploading. In that way, we can move past the prosaic concerns of brute technical capability and venture into the richer land of philosophical contemplation. Along similar lines, and perhaps unlike other books on this topic, this book does not speculate about, or otherwise attempt to predict, the timeline on which any technology will become viable. Concerns over the technological difficulty of brain-scanning, -freezing, or -slicing, or over nanobot construction, energy utilization, or actuation and movement, concerns over nanoscale engineering of artificial brains, or over

ting resources required for brain emulations—these kinds of
s are entirely unrelated to this book, as are any challenges re-
when (or if) such technologies could emerge. Such issues are
off topic with respect to the philosophical considerations. Many
other excellent resources are available which consider timelines of
technological evolution.

Note that we needn't necessarily fully understand how the brain
works in order to upload it [25]. This point is often missed as one frequently encounters arguments that mind-uploading is simply beyond
consideration until we have a complete understanding of how the
brain operates, both in its raw physiology and also in its metaphysical
effects, i.e., *how* the brain produces the mind. Neither of these concerns
is entirely valid (nor are they entirely invalid of course). Rather, we
need to get to the point in neurological science where we believe we
have a sufficient understanding to indicate at *which* physical level to
model the brain in order to replicate its mindful properties. Perhaps
that level is subatomic, implying that we must perfectly replicate individual quarks in a duplicate brain in order to invoke a duplicate (but
equivalent) mind. Perhaps the appropriate level is atomic, molecular,
neural, or event multi-neural (groups of neurons acting as a unit toward larger functionality, potentially collapsing thousands of neurons
into a single functional entity). In the extreme, we could model the entire brain as a single functional system and consequently consider any
artifact or emulation that replicates its external input/output functionality to be sufficient, regardless of how complex such a model would be
or how different the inner implementation of such a model would be
from natural neurology. This last position would essentially invoke *behavioral* philosophy, in which only external and observable organismal
behavior is of relevance to interpreting or judging the mindful properties of a brain, including identity and consciousness.

The point here is decidedly *not* to prescribe one of these system
levels (although to enable my exposition, I presume the appropriate
level is neural). Rather, the point is that once a level is chosen, we need
not necessarily understand the system below that level. We merely
need to replicate the brain's physical behavior at and above the pre-

scribed level of abstraction and the result will be deemed a sufficient model of the entire system. In line with the decision to rely on a neural level, simply to expedite the discussion, the system functionality in question then becomes the processing of afferent neural signals (incoming action potentials) and the production of efferent signals in accordance with observed biological systems.

This methodology is called *system identification*, whereby a researcher seeks to model some natural or dynamic system, settles upon some level of the system for his or her analysis, and assigns black-box status to the abstraction below that level, treating it as a form of signal input-output function whose internal workings are not only potentially unknown, but more importantly, are deemed *intrinsically irrelevant* to the larger model. In the case of modeling a brain and its mind, if one were to assume the appropriate level is neural, then, as a matter of policy, one could *entirely* disregard the minutiae of intracellular chemistry and merely focus on producing neural models that generate action potentials in response to patterns of received action potentials in a manner that statistically reflects natural neurons. If the reader balks at this suggestion that all intracellular chemistry can be utterly disregarded, then that does not indicate a failure of this approach, but merely rather that the reader prefers a lower level of abstraction, perhaps molecular. Crucially, *any* chosen level requires the same assumption: that all natural and/or physical processes below that level are irrelevant, possibly unknown or even unknowable. I have attempted to write this book to be compatible with any reader's preference in this regard.

System identification draws a line *below* which we can dispense with further physical or natural understanding, but what about higher levels of abstraction? I claimed above that we don't necessarily need to understand how the brain produces the mind in order to duplicate or emulate the mind via a second brain. This claim applies to incomplete knowledge on multiple levels: how do groups of neurons accomplish basic arithmetic computations? How do whole regions perform marvelous feats of processing, such as vision? Most abstractly, how does the overall brain give rise to cognition and emotion—or mind or consciousness? It is sometimes argued that until we fully understand how the brain produces the mind, we cannot even broach the topic of duplicating or emulating the brain's physical behavior with any expectation of capturing the higher phenomena too. There is a rationale for this challenge, but it is not unimpeachable. Rather, the willingness to dispense with a complete understanding of the brain-to-mind relationship requires that we adopt certain (hopefully reasonable) assumptions. For example, we must assume is that brain behavior is localized, either structurally or functionally (or both), i.e., that neurons communicate through a confined set of channels and that events outside those channels have no causal effect on neural behavior. The channels generally underlying this assumption are afferent dendritic action potentials and local chemical environments. This assumption of locality permits us to explicitly exclude all other issues and simply expect secondary phenomena to properly occur. Consider that, for most of history, the chemistry involved in the remarkable diversity and complexity of food preparation was a complete mystery. Ancient bakers and vintners had no idea *why* or *how* dough became bread, or grapes became wine (they almost surely didn't even realize yeast was alive!), but they knew that if they replicated a specific process, they would get a predictable (notably unintuitive) result. Their lack of understanding of how biological and molecular chemistry (to say nothing of atomic physics) enable dough to transmute into bread did not hinder their ability to perform basic practices and achieve predictable complex and indirect effects.

Another assumption that is crucial to deemphasizing a complete knowledge of brain and mind is that the higher phenomena of concern are *emergent*, i.e., that they occur in an implicit and automatic fashion from the local, individual behavior of their constituent parts. The premise of emergence is that once the individual components of a complex dynamic system have been established, the broader secondary phenomena will arise without further intent or intervention (much less comprehension); we just get those higher phenomena for free as an intrinsic property of the dynamic system. A reliance on emergence may seem like cheating, but it is straightforward in principle. My favorite example, flocking (discussed in some depth in this book), illustrates the idea. Once individual birds enact local behavioral rules of neighborly flight, the illusion of group-level coordination simply falls out of the system without further explanation. Thankfully, the notion that mind is emergent from the brain is not particularly contentious.

An admittedly strange feature of the organization this book employs is that it positions the glossary near the beginning. I don't consider the glossary to be merely supplemental or *reference* in nature (which would literally imply that the reader only *refers* to it occasionally as needed). Rather, I believe that one of the most important (and perplexingly challenging) aspects of communication is to first and foremost establish a shared vocabulary. Effective communication is particularly difficult when discussing an issue that straddles experimental science and armchair speculation, all the while spanning a spectrum of abstraction that reaches from fundamental metaphysical philosophy to unvarnished neurology. The generality and scope of this issue can't help but involve terms that share both technical and colloquial usage. Therefore, without precise definitions laid out in advance, any subsequent discussion will essentially be dead on arrival.

Some of my editors, whose opinions and advice I greatly respect, recommended I position the glossary in a more classical manner, at the end of the book. While I am sensitive to the undeniable rationale behind such a suggestion, I would be concerned that many readers would not refer to the glossary as needed, and consequently misunderstand those terms for which I rely upon somewhat unconventional definitions (e.g., consider the diversity and detail underlying the definition of *brain* in the glossary and as used throughout this book). At the same time, I realize that many readers will see a glossary at the beginning of a book as a barrier to smooth progress. As with other aspects of this book, I therefore ask the reader to work with me and appreciate that I am desperate to achieve concise communication concerning the topics I present. For those readers who can do the following, I recommend actually reading straight through the glossary as if it were prose. The type of philosopher (amateur or otherwise) who finds mind-uploading interesting in the first place should hopefully enjoy basking in the establishment of associated definitions anyway. On the other hand, for those readers who cannot withstand a brute glossary, perhaps skim it so as to hopefully trigger those words when you encounter them in the text, and then skip ahead to later sections and refer back as needed.

Following the glossary, I then offer, in chapter three, a second primarily referential section, wherein I present a taxonomy (a hierarchical, or mostly tree-like, classification) of speculative mind-uploading procedures that have cropped up over the years. Some can be attributed directly to particular people who introduced them in some clearly identifiable original source (perhaps a book). Some are commonly associated with science-fiction lore, calling upon recognizable exemplars from print or film but possibly without a specific origin in those archetypes. Most scenarios in the taxonomy, however, have arisen in a third way: in the fog of debate or personal musing as a direct response to earlier proposed mind-uploading scenarios for the express purpose of challenging or investigating philosophical conclusions that those earlier proposed procedures yielded. It is in this way that a taxonomy forms, with older and conceptually simpler scenarios residing higher in the taxonomy, and with derivations of increasing specificity hanging under them.

The taxonomy is relatively terse; it merely attempts to present and organize the various scenarios with minimal philosophical speculation or interpretation, and with a goal of minimizing contention with the reader. Although it is inevitable that many readers will take issue with some of the descriptions or the nature in which they are presented, the intent is nevertheless that any reader of any persuasion on various mind-uploading scenarios should be able to use the taxonomy as a testbed onto which to apply his or her personal views, i.e., to evaluate one's own philosophy against each item in the taxonomy.

As with the glossary, the taxonomy may make for somewhat laborious direct reading. Soldier on my good reader. If you find it tedious, skip ahead to section two and then merely drop back into the taxonomy either periodically and whimsically, or as a direct reference from later parts of the book that mention items within the taxonomy.

Section two is less referential and more philosophical. Chapters four and five take the reader through an end-to-end presentation from fundamental metaphysics to specific topics concerning brains and minds. Chapter six addresses some concerns I have over the notion of dualism, especially how it is used as an imprecise club in debates, and I consider some issues related to consciousness as a concept separate from minds. Chapter seven is the climax of the book, in which I state the primary thesis of how the various minds resulting from a mind-uploading procedure should be regarded in terms of their primacy to the original subject. Chapter eight is tangential, perhaps almost an appendix. It presents a relatively novel take on free-will with some curious implications for existentialism. Finally, in section three (chapter nine), I apply the philosophy as presented to several scenarios from the taxonomy to consider how this philosophy interprets various mind-uploading procedures.

~ 2 ~

Glossary

Please see the Introduction for an explanation as to why the glossary occurs at the beginning, rather than the end, of this book.

Debates on the topics surrounding mind-uploading get remarkably derailed over terminological preferences, such that the main issues of consideration become lost. Note that there are two potential levels of disagreement with which we must contend when considering a topic such as mind-uploading:

- Disagreements pertaining to the best definitions for the words included in such a glossary, i.e., disagreements concerning the glossary itself.
- Disagreements pertaining to fundamental philosophical challenges to the theories presented in later chapters.

Please don't confuse these two levels of potential disagreement. To get hung up on differences of opinion about how words should be defined is to miss the far more interesting potential topics of consideration and debate, the topics I myself find the most interesting.

Therefore, the following glossary establishes a set of definitions for various terms that are used throughout this book to discuss the nature of mind and the prospect of mind-uploading. At the same time, the glossary primarily serves to reduce miscommunication *within* this particular book, and not necessarily to establish global definitions that must attain broader usage, should the reader prefer it that way. This approach may come across as churlish, but it would be difficult to proceed otherwise for the simple fact that, as stated, many of the definitions required by these topics are themselves subject to considerable debate. Since a book, being a monodirectional conveyance from writer to reader, implicitly precludes any discussion or debate, I must simply settle upon a set of definitions and operate from that basis, for how else can I even broach the topic? I request enough compromise from the reader on this issue to enable forward progress on the larger philosophical questions which would otherwise be inaccessible.

The glossary is not organized alphabetically, but rather, incrementally, such that to the extent possible, terms whose definitions rely on other terms occur later in the glossary. Such an organization cannot be perfectly realized, but it is the primary organizing principle.

Mind:

1. A distinct (unique), identifiable (residing within some notion of boundary, probably nonspatio-temporal in nature), labelable (capable of being indicated relative to others) cognitive instance; a specific person for all intents and purposes. Note that the concept of *distinctiveness* is subject to some ambiguity: do two identical physical structures, necessarily non-unique (identical) albeit nevertheless separate in identity, indicate two fundamentally different things or merely two physical references to an otherwise single thing? This and related issues are covered in considerable depth in this book.

2. In metaphysical terms, within this book[2], a mind is a *type* composed of a sequence of *mind-state* types. See *type* and *mind-state*.

Dynamic: Undergoing state-change over time. Not tending to reside in an identical state from moment to moment. May apply to either physical or virtual structures. A dynamic system may be described as residing *within* time or as being temporal. Antonym: *nondynamic*.

Nondynamic/static: Exhibiting and experiencing no state-change over time. A nondynamic or static system may be described as residing *outside* of time or as being nontemporal. As such, operations or procedures on static systems may be performed at any conceivable rate with all associated results being interpretively identical (e.g., we can cut a solid cube of dead matter in half by moving the knife at any arbitrary speed, yet the resulting pieces, even the description of the overall system, will be identical in the end regardless of cutting rate). This property of nondynamicism or staticism has significant implications for the issue of gradualness, a concept of notable importance in many mind-uploading debates. Antonym: *dynamic*.

---

[2] In the interests of brevity, I won't overly repeat the disclaimer *"within this book"*. Please take it as a given.

Conscious/Consciousness: One of:

1. Essentially *wakefulness*. In this form, I often substitute the word *awake* with identical meaning. To be in a consciously awake state, a mind must be dynamic, experiencing the passage of time, such that ongoing and transpiring events may be observed and processed. As such, an awake mind may be described as *running* (in the way that we describe a computer program as *running* when it is operational, e.g., "*He ran the program*"). Unless explicitly stated otherwise, usage of *conscious* refers to this definition, not one of the other two. Antonym: *unconscious/asleep/anesthesia/coma*.

2. Immediate awareness of a particular cognitive activity, as contrasted with *subconscious(ness)* in which aspects of cognition occur without the *self* realizing, observing, or directing such activity. An example of these two concepts operating jointly would be writing, in which we are conscious of the content under construction but almost entirely subconscious of the rote actions of penmanship or typing. Another common example is walking, which we do while carrying on other complex activities with very little direct awareness even over rough ground. Yet deeper subconsciousness is often exemplified by subliminal advertising, hypnosis (questionable), or various automatic motor systems like breathing, pulse or eye-blinking (which one can become painfully conscious of as a result of a trigger, as this passage may have just done to you. Sorry).

3. The nearly ineffable mental state or experience generally associated with the term consciousness. I prefer not to offer a specific definition here since nearly everyone prefers their own definition on the matter. The reader can find copious resources on the topic elsewhere [7, 13, 30, 41]. Crucially, I don't consider this usage of the term very much (except in chapter 6), since, for the most part, I consider this usage essentially synonymous with *mind* with respect to the uploading question. See *mind*.

Unconscious/asleep/anesthesia/coma: These four terms may be used interchangeably within the scope of the primary topic at hand. That is to say, their physiological differences are irrelevant within the scope of this book. The salient features of unconsciousness are:

1. Static structure (the substrate's structure, either physical or virtual, does not change over time). This is admittedly a pretty severe departure from the general use of these terms since none of the physiological meanings of unconsciousness, sleep, etc. imply utterly static physical structure, but rather merely imply various cognitive levels of nonfunctionality.
2. Unawareness of the passage of the time and the inability to observe or process any ongoing circumstances.
3. Relatedly, the complete lack of sensory phenomena, such that no events in the surrounding environment may causally affect the internal state of the mind.

Antonym: *conscious/consciousness (def 1).*

Subjective perspective (sometimes point-of-view or POV): A mind's experience of self-identity, its awareness of its surroundings, circumstances, and location within those surroundings and circumstances; the processing of such circumstances to make sense of the mind's own place in, and unique perception of, the (or *a*) world.

Biological: Explicitly the biological tissues, etc. that make up the human brain, with an emphasis on neurons. Antonym: *artificial.*

Nanobot/Nanorobot: A neuron-like robot (in terms of scale, structure, and functionality). Note that both within and outside this book, the term nanobot frequently describes devices that approximate cellular scales. In such cases, the *nano* qualifier refers not to the size of the device itself, but to the scale of precision of its parts.

Computerized: One of three things, all variations on physical computer-like devices:

1. A nanobot, namely intended to replicate neural function, primarily accumulating afferent dendritic signals, processing a threshold function, and emitting efferent axonal signals. If deemed necessary, nanobots could optionally incorporate microtubule-like quantum phenomena.

2. A composition of such nanobots into a complete brain. The network topology need not perfectly reflect a source biological brain, although it certainly could. Alternatively, it might merely instantiate the required network architecture to emulate or replicate the higher-level functionality of a brain. Such abstracted topology might first be determined via software emulations and only later be converted to a physical nanobot network.

3. A somewhat conventional macroscopic computer on which a simulation or emulation of a brain is run. The nature of such a computer is left unspecified, including parallelism, electronic vs. photonic vs. magnetic storage and transmission, etc. Even the possibility of quantum computation is left open to interpretation.

Virtual: A software simulation or emulation, either of a physical system or of abstract functional behavior. Antonym: *physical*.

Physical: A system whose primary properties are essentially material in nature, not simulated or emulated. Antonym: *virtual*.

Artificial: Either computerized or virtual, but not biological. This term is used when the distinction between computerized and virtual is unimportant to the statement. Antonym: *biological*.

Structure/structural: Concerning a physical, simulated-physical or emulated-physical spatial arrangement of material parts, generally parts of the brain. Antonym: *functional*.

Functional (sometimes behavioral): Concerning the operational characteristics of a system as opposed to its component characteristics; often focused on the correlations (and possible causations) between inputs and outputs of a system. Antonym: *structural.*

Brain:
1. A system that produces a mind (please see figure 2 for further clarification). Major classifications include:
    1. Physical biological brain: The biological organ commonly accepted to be the substrate of, and whose behavior produces in an unspecified way, a mind. Materialism and related philosophies hold that the brain is sufficient to produce a mind, i.e., that a *soul* or other supernatural and non-brain-associated entity, is not required.
    2. Physical computerized brain: A physical structure that closely mimics the neuron/synapse structure of a biological brain, essentially billions of nano-scale computational units networked together in a design comparable to a biological brain. Note that theories of mind that require intracellular quantum phenomena are not precluded here since computerized brains could include comparable quantum processes [17].
    3. Virtual structural brain: A three-dimensional software simulation or emulation of the spatial neuron/synapse structure and function of a biological brain.
    4. Virtual functional brain: A software simulation of the functional behavior of a neuron/synapse structure without regard for spatial relationships, essentially a typical contemporary neural network system as is common in artificial intelligence and machine learning research.

5. Virtual higher-order brain: A software simulation of the higher-order cognitive algorithms often otherwise encoded by lower-order neural structures, e.g., receptive fields, cortical columns, frequency filter banks, Gabor wavelets, etc. Some theories of mind may consider an artificial brain operating at a higher-order level of abstraction to be sufficient to both capture and run a mind.

2. In metaphysical terms, a *brain* is a *type* composed of a sequence of *brain-state* types. See *type* and *brain-state*.

Substrate: The system which operationalizes (runs/performs) the functionality of a brain, i.e., the system necessary to produce a mind. While straightforward in the case of a biological or computerized brain, substrate becomes ambiguous with respect to virtual brains: is the substrate the physical hardware computing the simulation or is the substrate the simulated structure or neuron-functional abstraction itself? Substrates can be classified in several ways, which group the five brain types at a sliding cutoff of functional abstraction:

	Functional abstraction cutoff	Brain types A	Brain types B
1	Biological vs. computerized	[1]	[2, 3, 4, 5]
2	Physical vs. virtual	[1, 2]	[3, 4, 5]
3	Structural vs. functional	[1, 2, 3]	[4, 5]
4	Neural vs. higher-order	[1, 2, 3, 4]	[5]

Table 1. Grouping of brain classifications based on functional abstraction of substrate – This table shows how the five brain classifications (see *brain*) can be divided at a sliding cutoff based on the functional abstraction of their underlying substrate. See figure 2 for more information.

Gradualism: A dynamic process in which the overall rate of change does not exceed some designated maximum tolerable rate. Gradualism can apply (or fail to apply) to either temporally continuous or discontinuous (aka, discrete) processes; the concepts of gradualism and temporal continuity are not necessarily correlated. Note that there may be considerable debate over what rate qualifies as the gradualism threshold for any given process.

Temporal continuity: A dynamic process in which state pairs occurring adjacent in time by some designated *small* window of time differ by no more than some designated *sufficiently-small* delta. Similarly, temporal continuity implies that such differences are not considered intolerably *step-wise*. Note that this definition does not require a perfectly analog process, but rather tolerates discreteness below a designated threshold. For example, gradual replacement upload procedures tolerate structural replacement at some unit feature-level (neural, synaptic, possibly even molecular), but are nevertheless generally considered continuous when contrasted with alternatives, such as scan-and-copy procedures. Temporal continuity should not be confused with gradualism. These two concepts can occur in all four boolean combinations. Antonym: *temporal discontinuity/discreteness*.

Temporal discontinuity/Discreteness (sometimes step-wise): A dynamic process in which state pairs occurring adjacent in time differ by an amount that exceeds some designated tolerance of continuity. Similarly, discreteness implies that such differences are considered *step-wise*. Antonym: *temporal continuity*.

Running: For a mind to be conscious or awake; to be in a state in which a brain and its mind are dynamic, cognitively processing their ongoing circumstances. Antonym: *frozen*.

Frozen: A catch-all term for various technologies by which, and scenarios under which, a brain is put into an unconscious state, i.e., static. The term is not necessarily meant to be taken literally, although temperature-associated *freezing* (aka, cryogenics/cryonics) is certainly part of the repertoire. For example, in the case of a nonphysical brain, a frozen state simply implies that its computational hardware is not *running*. Antonym: *running*.

Uploading procedure: A hypothetical procedure, ostensibly somewhat medical in nature, involving the two part process of first, scanning the structure or functional behavior of a biological brain, and second, subsuming and replacing, or duplicating, the scanned structure or scanned functionality in a second instance, often a different substrate. Uploading procedures broadly fall into two categories, with numerous gradations of increasing granularity:

1. In-place replacement: the scan and replacement process occurs within the skull on a microscopic level at some prescribed feature-scale, often neuronal, but not necessarily. The goal is clearly not to transfer the mind to a new location, but rather to replace the biological components (neurons) with artificial components, e.g., computerized nanobots.

2. Scan-and-duplicate: the resulting upload's hardware rarely resides within the biological brain's skull. Generally divided into the following secondary categories:

   1. Destructive: The scanning process requires destroying the biological brain.

   2. Nondestructive: The scanning process can be accomplished without harming the brain, leaving open the possibility that multiple minds result from the procedure, the original and one or more uploads.

While seemingly straightforward as a first-order classification, the taxonomy presented in chapter 3 challenges the boundaries of these simple categories (as well as deeper categories). Note that the concept of an uploading procedure makes no claim as to the procedure's philosophical success in the ostensible goal of transferring the mind; it merely describes the technical aspects of the procedure. Qualitative analysis falls under term of *mind-uploading*.

Subject/patient: These terms are used interchangeably to indicate the biological brain (and its mind and its person) undergoing an uploading procedure. Sometimes used even more generally to refer to any mind resulting from such a procedure, even an uploaded mind.

System Identification: The process of modeling a dynamic system by observing the statistical properties of its input and output data channels (or just its output data if input data is inaccessible). When conducted using *black box* techniques, the internal functionality of the system is not necessarily discovered during modeling. Rather, merely an abstraction of its input/output function is deduced. See *whole brain emulation*.

Mind-Uploading (MU): Multiple not-necessarily-compatible definitions. Specifically, an *uploading procedure* by which:
1. Any uploaded minds have the subjective perspective of having transferred from a biological brain and body to a new (usually artificial) substrate.
2. The uploaded mind intrinsically *transfers* from the original substrate to the new substrate, regardless of the various subjective perspectives of the subjects involved.

Colloquially, the biological brain (and its mind) is often labeled the *original* and any new brains (and their minds) are often labeled as either uploads, clones, copies, or duplicates. However, these terms (with the exception of upload) are not preferred because their biased connotations insinuate a priori primary and subsidiary status, thereby undermining subsequent philosophical analysis. This book will, for the most part, simply refer to the biological brain and its mind, and to the upload and its artificial brain.

Substrate-Independent Minds (SIM):[3] The objective to be able to sustain person-specific functions of mind and experience in many different operational substrates besides the biological brain. A mind becomes substrate-independent in a manner analogous to that by which platform-independent code can be compiled and run on many different computing platforms.

Whole Brain Emulation (WBE): The approach to SIM that is most closely based on current neuroscience methods, particularly reverse engineering in terms of neuroanatomy and neurophysiology, using the procedure of *system identification* to emulate brain mechanisms that give rise to functions of mind.

Upload:
1. (verb): To perform a mind-uploading procedure.
2. (noun): Any mind resulting from an uploading procedure that does not arise from the biological brain that *entered* the procedure.

Cloning: Cloning does not imply the modern scientific process of producing a genetically identical organism, but rather the (currently) fictional mind-uploading procedure in which both the original and the upload are biological brains. In cloning, the upload may also be referred to as a clone.

---

[3] Thanks to Randal Koene for providing definitions for SIM and WBE. Please visit www.carboncopies.org, www.minduploading.org, www.wholebrainemulation.org, and www.substrateindependentminds.org for more information.

Spatial continuity: Existence in (or direct association with) a spatial domain such that discontinuous transformations (usually translations) through space do not occur. When applied to physical objects, spatial continuity implies the absence of *teleportation* while spatial discontinuity implies disjunct translation through space, aka, teleportation. Teleportation is generally considered as applied to physical objects, i.e., objects that disappear from one location and appear in another. However, the term can apply to abstract entities, or even *functionality*, such as minds and mental function, if those entities are first *assigned* to a physical location (or are assigned a tight association with some physical object, perhaps minds to brains). In such a case, spatially continuous properties then apply to such abstract phenomena as well. Where such nonphysical phenomena are indelibly linked to physical objects, their respective spatial discontinuities are synonymous. Antonym: *spatial discontinuity*.

Spatial discontinuity: Existence in (or direct association with) a spatial domain such that discontinuous transformations (usually translations) through space may occur. When applied to physical objects, spatial discontinuity implies the possibility of *teleportation*. When applied to nonphysical phenomena, spatial discontinuity implies that such phenomena may *transfer* between spatial locations or object ownership. Whether such a system is deemed tolerable for the purposes of some goal (e.g., mind-uploading) depends highly on the philosophies applied. For example, functionalism and related philosophies may accommodate spatial discontinuity of nonphysical phenomena, depending on one's precise views. This book considers this issue in great detail. Antonym: *spatial continuity*.

Determinism (Physical Determinism): The philosophical position that if a physical system were allowed to operate from the same initial state multiple times, it would undergo an identical dynamic evolution, thereby exhibiting identical intermediate states at any given delta-time after the start time. Determinism is often considered to be incompatible with free-will, although an alternative interpretation is offered in this book.

Free-will: The philosophical position that minds can exhibit genuine *choice* (freedom) beyond the rote behavior of either their underlying physical structure, genetic inclination, or psychological drives (in some circles, these three concepts represent three significantly different approaches to the issue). Similarly, free-will can refer to the position that epiphenomena (mind) may causally influence primary phenomena (physical events). Free-will is often considered difficult to reconcile with physical determinism (although the philosophy of *compatiblism* specifically aims to allow both to be true at the same time). This book offers a fairly novel approach to free-will.

Information: Either the Shannon information of a bit string, or the closely related notion of the Kolmogorov complexity of a bit string.

Entropy: Entropy as it is is associated with both thermodynamics, and more fundamentally, with information theory.

Spatial: Residing in (embedded within) one or more spatial dimensions, almost always three dimensions. Antonym: *abstract/abstraction*.

Temporal: Residing in (embedded within) a time dimension. Experiencing dynamic processes, i.e., state changes over time. Antonym: *abstract/abstraction*. If an object is static, it is not considered to be temporal even if it *physically exists*, e.g., an inanimate chunk of matter is not meaningfully a temporal entity, although it is still clearly spatial.

Spatio-temporal: Residing in (embedded within) both a spatial and a temporal dimension. Although the dimensionality of the spatial component need not be specified, it is generally assumed to be three-dimensional. As per the definition of temporal, a spatio-temporal object is implicitly dynamic. Otherwise, it is simply spatial. Antonym: *abstract/abstraction*.

Abstract/abstraction: Residing in neither spatial nor temporal *dimensions*. This concept applies to metaphysical *universals*, *types*, and some, but not all, *occurrences*. Antonym: *particular, spatio-temporal*.

Particular: In metaphysics, an instantiated or embedded *universal*, a single entity, even if other identical instances also exist. Opinions differ as to whether particulars must be spatio-temporal (essentially tokens) or whether they can be abstract (essentially occurrences). In either case, the term is redundant with either *token* or *occurrence*, and as such will not be used in this book. It is only included in this glossary because it is often one half of a dichotomy with *universals* and therefore should be included for completeness. Antonym: *universal*.

Universal: In metaphysics, the qualities or characteristics that may apply to *particulars* (aka, *tokens* or *occurrences*). There are three kinds:
1. Types: multi-item groupings (or recognized *kinds*) of shared identity, e.g., red things[4], sharp things.
2. Properties: single-item qualities, e.g., redness or sharpness.
3. Relations: two-item inequalities, e.g., redder, sharper.
Only *types* are discussed in this book.

---

[4] See footnote in section *Universals, Realism, Tokens, Occurrences* with respect to Chalmers' and Dennett's probable objection.

Type: One of the three kinds of metaphysical universal qualities or characteristics, focusing on the quality of object-grouping based on similar labeled identity, e.g., birds, planets, sentences, numerals (i.e., digit sequences). Sometimes the notion of *group* is replaced with the notion of *kind*. This distinction is a relatively significant question within metaphysical philosophy.

Occurrence: An embedded or instantiated *type*. The notion of occurrence is a set consisting to two nonoverlapping strict subsets: *tokens* and *abstract occurrences*.

Token: A spatio-temporal *occurrence* of a *type*, e.g., a typical physical object. Tokens are a strict subset of occurrences (all tokens are occurrences). Tokens are always spatial and generally temporal, although some nontemporal examples are presented in this book.

Abstract Occurrence (possibly trope): A nonspatio-temporal *occurrence* of a *type*. Abstract occurrences are a strict subset of occurrences. A common example is individual numbers which instantiate an associated numeral type. For example, the number 123 is a numeral type, while specific instances of that type, such as occur in the equation (123 + 456) or in the address *123 Elm Street*, are abstract occurrences of the numeral. Likewise, a physical (i.e., spatial) instance of the equation or address contains a 123 token (e.g., ink on paper, light on a computer display, chiseled into stone, etc.). Some philosophers use the term *trope* to indicate a fairly similar concept. I am honestly not certain if the concept of tropes is identical or merely related to abstract occurrences. As such, I won't use the term.

Platonic realism: The philosophical position that universals exist in their own right, that they truly exist regardless of any connection (or lack thereof) to physical reality. A Platonic realist would say we *discover* types. Contrast with Aristotelian realism.

Aristotelian realism: The philosophical position that universals only exist as dependent on and associated with the occurrences that embed them. An Aristotelian realist would say we *create* types when we create tokens that exhibit their description (and presumably that we destroy them in an opposing fashion). Contrast with Platonic realism.

Mind-state: Other philosophers have used this term to indicate a single mental concept, like *seeing a cat* or *feeling a pain*. It is used differently in this book however, to describe the entire mental phenomena of a mind (a person) at a given moment in time (a point in that person's life). In metaphysical terms, a *type* representing the totality of mental phenomena that represent a mind at a given moment in time, i.e., the innate cognitive features, in addition to the life-long accumulated experiences and memories, of a mind from birth until a given moment in that mind's (that person's) life. Mind-states are isomorphic with brain-states. A sequence of mind-states is a mind. Mind-states are definitively nonspatio-temporal so they cannot be instantiated as tokens, but they can occur as *abstract occurrences*, namely in direct association with a tokenized brain-state (i.e., a brain).

Brain-state: In metaphysical terms, a *type* representing the material state of a biological brain at a given moment in time. The physical resolution is not prescribed in this book (it could possibly be as high-level as cortical columns or as low-level as subatomic particles). Brain-states are isomorphic with mind-states. A token of a brain-state is generally a biological brain, although the concept could conceivably apply to various kinds of artificial brains.

~ 3 ~

Taxonomy of
Mind-Uploading Scenarios

This chapter presents a taxonomy of sorts, organizing various mind-uploading procedures that have arisen over the years, in addition to a few new additions which emerged naturally during my development of the taxonomy. The taxonomy is organized hierarchically such that outer (or upper) levels are so abstract as to not fully qualify as actual scenarios, but rather merely categorize scenarios presented in lower levels. Intermediate levels present specific scenarios, but only describe their more basic traits, and consequently merely restate popular scenarios which have been contemplated by others in the past. Lower levels derive from their parent scenario, either by creating a new (or altered) scenario, or by clarifying in greater detail the parameters of the parent scenario, to see if earlier conclusions withstand deeper scrutiny. In most cases, a derived scenario is specifically designed to stress-test one particular conclusion (or reason for a conclusion) that may have been drawn from its parent scenario. As such, most scenarios implicitly suggest a few specific questions as to how the new traits, or the more precisely described traits, might impact the earlier conclusions. Note that throughout this book, the numerous scenarios included in the taxonomy are referred to using the § symbol.

As mentioned in the introduction, I concede that this chapter may make for somewhat tedious reading due to its referential nature. While I have attempted to present the taxonomy in a readable manner, should the reader find the journey to be getting lost in the brush, he or she should feel free to skip to later chapters, and merely refer back to the taxonomy from the later discussions.

Please bear the following disclaimer in mind: Throughout this chapter, I often write as if it is generally assumed that the structural and functional level of the brain which must be adequately modeled and/or artificially replaced in an upload is the neuron. This is shorthand, however. To advance the exposition without continually distracting disclaimers, I simply assume that individual neurons are the granular unit in question. The reader is more than welcome to extend this assumption arbitrarily to suit his or her philosophical preference. For those who think the necessary level of neurological behavior is the synapse, simply read *synapse* where I have written *neuron*. For those who believe various intracellular structures, molecular arrangements (proteins perhaps), or even nanoscale quantum-physical microtubules [17], are required in a model in order to successfully *capture* a mind, perform the necessary substitution as you read. Alternatively, some readers may believe that we don't even need to delve as deep as the neuron, but rather merely to some larger neural configuration (receptive fields or cortical columns perhaps, just to name two examples). Go with whatever floats your boat, or your thought experiment, as the case may be. One thorn in such extrapolations is that in some places, I offer explicit calculations which assume the total number of structural or functional units is 100 billion since I have taken the neuron to be the crucial unit. If the reader prefers a different physical structure as the basic component, he or she will have to adapt the math accordingly.

Index

1. GRADUAL REPLACEMENT PROCEDURES

1.1.   Essentially-in-place procedures
  1.1.1.   In-place destructive procedures
    1.1.1.1.   In-place destructive conscious nanobot replacement
      1.1.1.1.1.   Spectrum of temporal rates
        1.1.1.1.1.1.   Neurons / second (n/s)
        1.1.1.1.1.2.   Neuron-batches
      1.1.1.1.2.   Spectrum of spatial displacements
      1.1.1.1.3.   Nondestructive brain-doubling
      1.1.1.1.4.   Delayed destructive brain-doubling
    1.1.1.2.   In-place destructive frozen nanobot replacement
      1.1.1.2.1.   Temporal discontinuity
      1.1.1.2.2.   Spatial discontinuity
      1.1.1.2.3.   Frozen nondestructive brain-doubling
  1.1.2.   In-place nondestructive procedures
    1.1.2.1.   In-place nondestructive conscious nanobot brain-doubling
      1.1.2.1.1.   Brain-doubling with temporary biological shutdown
        1.1.2.1.1.1.   Spatial translation
      1.1.2.1.2.   In-place delayed destructive conscious nanobot replacement
    1.1.2.2.   In-place nondestructive frozen brain-doubling
      1.1.2.2.1.   Spatial discontinuity
1.2.   Non-in-place procedures
  1.2.1.   Moravec bush-robot
    1.2.1.1.   Nondestructive bush-robot with temporary biological shutdown
    1.2.1.2.   Multi-armed bush-robot

2. SCAN-AND-DUPLICATE PROCEDURES

2.1.   Frozen scan-and-copy procedures
  2.1.1.   Frozen destructive scan-and-copy
    2.1.1.1.   Physical biological brain
    2.1.1.2.   Physical computerized brain
    2.1.1.3.   Virtual structural brain
    2.1.1.4.   Virtual functional brain
    2.1.1.5.   Virtual higher-order brain
  2.1.2.   Frozen nondestructive scan-and-copy
    2.1.2.1.   Both brains are awakened in naturally varying sensory environments
    2.1.2.2.   Both brains are awakened in essentially identical sensory environments

2.1.2.3.   Both brains are awakened in identical sensory environments in a deterministic universe: The White Room
2.2.   Conscious scan-and-copy procedures
  2.2.1.   Conscious destructive
    2.2.1.1.   Conscious destructive scan-and-copy with instantaneous scan: Teleportation
    2.2.1.2.   Conscious destructive scan-and-copy with noninstantaneous scan
  2.2.2.   Conscious nondestructive
    2.2.2.1.   Conscious nondestructive scan-and-copy with instantaneous scan
      2.2.2.1.1.   Nonidentical setting for the upload's reception
      2.2.2.1.2.   Identical setting with respect to sensory input
    2.2.2.2.   Conscious nondestructive scan-and-copy with noninstantaneous scan

3. BRAIN DIVISION PROCEDURES

3.1.   Divide brain at 50%
3.2.   Divide at 1%
3.3.   Divide at 51%
3.4.   Divide at 33% 3 times
3.5.   Divide at 1% 100 times
3.6.   Divide at 1/100-billionth
3.7.   Divide at 1/100-billionth 100 billion times

Detail

1. **GRADUAL REPLACEMENT SCENARIOS** – These procedures almost always produce a computerized brain, not a virtual brain. The basic process common to all procedures of this type is that the biological brain is replaced part-for-part with a computerized equivalent. Many variables are left unspecified, such as the required structural granularity (are the *parts* that are steadily replaced neurons, molecular-scale structures, microtubular- or atomic-scale structures, or possible larger multi-neuron multi-cell groupings, or even whole *brain regions* with an aim toward black box behavioral functionality?) Another unspecified variable is the interpretation of the word *gradual*. What replacement rate is gradual enough to maintain conscious continuity? Or to state the reverse, what rate of transfer is too fast to tolerate (meaning that we would not consider the upload procedure to successfully maintain identity as opposed to *killing and replacing* the subject)? Of the various uploading procedures commonly contemplated, gradual procedures, especially gradual *in-place* procedures (this point is scrutinized below) are often the most palatable in that, depending on one's philosophical stance, they can appear to resolve a fundamental problem where scan-and-duplicate procedures may fail, namely, does the original mind successfully transfer to the artificial brain? I propose alternative interpretations later, but it is certainly true that many people who are troubled by scan-and-duplicate procedures find gradual in-place replacement procedures far more acceptable. Of course, some people don't even consider gradual in-place uploading to be viable and believe that the original mind dies as a result of virtually any procedure. Such conclusions essentially exclude mind-uploading in principle.

1.1. **Essentially-in-place procedures** – Most people may believe that all gradual replacement procedures are inherently in-place procedures, that is, procedures in which each neuron of the actual biological brain is replaced by a computerized substitute in its own location inside the skull (although I scrutinize in-placeness in §1.1.1.1.2). Interestingly, one of the oldest and best-described procedures violates this assumption, but has not survived well in the contemporary zeitgeist and therefore may be unknown to younger or less-informed readers. I present it in §1.2 below. This section initially considers procedures in which the actual skull cavity is gradually evacuated of its biological brain (with some exceptions explored) and equally gradually filled with a computerized brain.

1.1.1. In-place destructive procedures – In-place procedures in which the original brain is destroyed as a result. This is by far the more commonly considered in-place scenario, the nondestructive alternative being so alien that I suspect very few people are even conceptually aware of it (presented in §1.1.2).

1.1.1.1. In-place destructive conscious nanobot replacement – This is one of the most common mind-uploading scenarios. A destructive procedure implies that the biological brain is destroyed. A conscious procedure implies that the brain is in a dynamic and waking state throughout the procedure. Nanobot replacement is the canonical in-place replacement method for such procedures. The basic idea consists of cellular-scale robots (commonly referred to as nanobots, named for the scale of their constituent parts, not their overall size) that take residence near (attached to?) single assigned neurons, model their assigned neurons until achieving satisfactory replicability of function, then kill the neurons, attach to their synaptic connections, and subsume their functionality with neither upstream nor downstream neurons being *aware* that the substitution has occurred (i.e., sensing or behaving differently as a consequence of their neighbor's artificial replacement). In the spirit of the approximate temporal continuity and gradualism often associated with this procedure, the nanobots are assumed to replace their assigned neurons one by one over some sufficiently lengthy period of time, thereby allowing the overall brain to steadily accommodate the new artificial structure in a continuous and smooth manner[5]. However, what this replacement rate should be, or what a maximum acceptable rate would be, are rarely specified in detail (see §1.1.1.1.1). Note that this procedure implicitly involves a certain (commonly unappreciated) nonzero spatial displacement of neural function from a cell to the nearby nanobot. Even if the nanobot is literally attached to the cell, this displacement of function still approximates cellular scales (5–100 microns). That is to say that the functional behavior of the neuron, its computation, its neural or cognitive *work*, undergoes a spatially discontinuous jump from the neuron to the nanobot at the moment the nanobot enacts its command to kill and replace the neuron. The neural function doesn't translate smoothly through space; rather it is being performed in one location and then a moment later it is being performed in a slightly offset location, with no smooth transition in between (see §1.1.1.1.2). Curiously, these displacements accumulate up to ~500km to ~10,000km of discontinuous spatial transfer of neural function over the entire upload (5–100 microns × 100 billion neurons). This fact that spatially discontinuous transfer of neural function indisputably occurs is extremely germane to the thought experiment since this method is often specifically lauded for its claim to maintaining unassailable spatial continuity, which simply isn't true. To those readers who, upon reading this section, don't understand what the big deal is, realize that to many other people, the issue of spatial continuity is a critical, even deal-breaking, aspect of mind-uploading analysis. The only reason the accumulated distance doesn't translate into a lateral transfer of the resulting computerized brain is that rather than being synchronized all in one direction, it consists of numerous uncoordi-

---

[5] Note that the popular concept that the brain needs time to *adapt* to the ongoing replacement fundamentally implies that the procedure is not, in fact, perfect. Such imperfection is precisely what the brain is apparently adapting to, but at the same time, implied imperfection clearly precludes any illusion that the replacement is perfect to begin with. Rather, such reasoning essentially requires that the nanobots not actually perfectly replicate their neurons. Such a proposition wouldn't generally be popular with many proponents of this procedure; the pervading tone is that perfect replacement is crucial to overall success. Contrarily, if we believe that sufficient replication within the tolerances of the procedure is achievable to begin with, then no *adaptation* phase is required and we can logically complete the global replacement essentially instantaneously with a final interpretation of *successful transfer*. It's difficult to have it both ways on this issue.

nated jumps that buzz around in a wild swarm within the skull cavity. It is difficult to understand why this distinction should grant the scenario a judgement of success where a mono-directional jump would be deemed to fail.

1.1.1.1.1. **Spectrum of temporal rates** – We can investigate §1.1.1.1 in greater detail by considering the spectrum of temporal rates that might be employed, as explored in the next two sections.

1.1.1.1.1.1. **Neurons/second (n/s)** – We can express the rate of a gradual upload in n/s, such that no two neurons upload at precisely the same instant no matter how fast the overall procedure might be. Expressed in this way, there is no technical lower bound to the rate, i.e., we can go as slowly as we like. However, we can prescribe some reasonable lower bounds. For example, 10,000 n/s would yield a total upload time of ~100 days, which is probably the slowest continual invasive medical procedure we can realistically expect any patient to tolerate. 100,000 n/s would yield a total upload time of ten days and 1,000,000 n/s would require one day. The upper bound on this rate asymptotically approaches a simultaneous, instantaneous upload: infinity n/s. A rate of 100 billion n/s would complete the procedure in one second. It is worth noting how high these seemingly reasonable rates are. Readers who are principally comfortable with the concept of gradual uploading may perceive it as being a rather languid procedure, allowing the brain plenty of time to accommodate the replaced neurons. In truth, if we consider that neuron processing speeds top out at around 100 action potentials per second (and *far* slower for most neurons), then an upload rate of 10,000 n/s (the slowest rate offered above) would kill and replace 100 neurons between temporally adjacent action potentials. This observation raises the question of just how *gradual* this procedure really is, since the hallmark of gradual procedures is their ability to steadily incorporate and adapt to the newly replaced neurons as they come online (how does the brain steadily accommodate hundreds or even thousands of neurons instantly uploading between adjacent action potentials?). One solution is to dispense with any cutoff in tolerable replacement rate and accept the final upload as genuine (as housing the original mind) across the full spectrum of conceivable rates. Such an interpretation would minimize the potential arbitrariness or other potential logical inconsistencies that may be associated with assigning a cutoff. Alternatively, perhaps some particular cutoff can, in fact, be rationally defended.

1.1.1.1.1.2. **Neuron-batches** – We can express the rate of a gradual upload as a series of discrete upload batches and an associated recovery period between batches. Each batch consists of some number of neurons that are simultaneously killed and replaced by their associated nanobots. The batch size can be indicated either as a specific number of neurons or as a percent of the brain (which of course, directly, if loosely, translates into a number of neurons). The primary questions are: what is the maximum tolerable batch size and the minimum tolerable recovery period to maintain the original mind through-out the process? Additionally, there may be a trade-off in which larger batches can be tolerated with a longer recovery period. If this trade-off is linear (twice the batch size requiring twice the recovery period), then the overall upload time will not be affected and we need only decide upon (or far better yet, objectively determine) the upper-bound on tolerable batch size and lower-bound on tolerable recovery period. When contemplating these issues, every effort should be made to offer rational arguments for the chosen bounds. A batch size of one (a single neuron) is implicitly tolerable, as it is synonymous with a conventional gradual upload procedure, §1.1.1.1, but should a batch size of a mere two neurons be deemed intrinsically intolerable, so as to assume it would kill the patient? If not two, then what is the upper bound? 1000 neurons/batch? 100,000 neurons/batch? .0001% of the brain/batch? 1%? How could we designate these cutoffs objectively? Ultimately, will the derived upper-bounds on batch size and lower-bounds on recovery period permit an over-all upload time that is within reason (probably less than a year, preferably on the scale of days)?

1.1.1.1.2. **Spectrum of spatial displacements** – We can investigate this procedure in greater detail by considering the spectrum of per-neuron spatial displacements within which we consider the procedure to maintain continuity of the running mind (initially presented in §1.1.1.1). Many people would argue that no spatial displacement of any degree is tolerable, but it was shown in §1.1.1.1 that the true lower-bound cannot possibly be zero, but rather in the range of 5–100 microns per neuron and 500km-10,000km accumulated over the procedure; true spatial continuity is simply impossible, despite popular claims to the contrary. The upper-bound on spatial displacement is the distance over which operational connectivity can be maintained. We can estimate this distance from the respective rates of neural-signal transmission and analogous computerized electrical or optical transmission. I will dispense with the subtle differences between nonsuper-conducting and super-conducting electricity, much less theoretical optical-computing systems; the truth is that the variation in speeds these systems would offer is well within the precision of the estimate itself. For an initial estimate, I will assume the speed of transmission within and between our computerized replacement nanobots approximates the speed of light, ~300 million m/s. Speed is an indication of a signal channel's latency, or the delay from transmitting a bit until it is received elsewhere. The bandwidth of a signal pertains to how many bits can be emitted by a source and disambiguated by a receiver in a given time. Computer bandwidths are on the order of millions or even billions of bits per second (Hertz, or Hz). Analogous biological rates are *much* slower. Action potential (AP) conduction speeds vary between 10 m/s and 100 m/s [28] (with extreme examples peaking upwards of 120 m/s). AP emission frequencies are comparable, around 10–100 Hz (this is, of course, a numerical coincidence since the choice of meters as the unit of distance is entirely arbitrary). So we can say neural transmissions exhibit speeds of 10–100m/s and rates of 10–100 AP/s (aka, Hz). Comparing the computerized and neural rates, we then derive a factor-3-million difference in transmission speed (latency) and a factor-10-million difference in frequency (bandwidth). Clearly, we must operate within the bounds of the lower estimate, so we will take factor-3-million as our final estimate. However, I would like to accommodate the fact that I set the upper-bound on computerized speeds at the speed of light, which may be too fast. Furthermore, I feel that the least precisely indicated figure was the computerized bandwidth; it could reasonably be quite lower. To account for these variances, and preferring to confine my estimate to a simple power of ten, I will assume the factor difference in question is one million. This final estimate, this ratio of one million to one, translates directly into a feasible increase in distance over which unimpeded connectivity should be maintainable between a replacement nanobot and its connected nonuploaded neurons (or with other adjacent nanobots). In other words, a nanobot can replace a neuron and subsequently communicate with its upstream and downstream counterparts with full neural functionality from a distance one million times further from those counterparts than the original neuron could manage. Neural spacing is reasonably approximated by their actual size, which as stated is on the order of 5–100 microns. The factor-1-million difference then yields an offset of ~5 million – 100 million microns (5m–100m). From this we may conclude that the minimum and maximum spatial discontinuity tolerances for a conventional *in-place* upload are no less than 5–100 microns due to neuron-nanobot adjacency, and conceivably as high as 5–100 meters on the theory that within that range, the replacement nanobots could maintain proper neural function with their connected counterparts.

1.1.1.1.3. Nondestructive brain-doubling – Please see §1.1.2.1 (*in-place nondestructive conscious nanobot brain-doubling*). This scenario is only listed here since it is a philosophical extension of *in-place destructive conscious nanobot replacement*, but is located in the taxonomy based on its procedural classification.

1.1.1.1.4. Delayed destructive brain-doubling – Please see §1.1.2.1.2 (*in-place delayed destructive conscious nanobot replacement*). This scenario is only listed here since it is a philosophical extension of *in-place destructive conscious nanobot replacement*, but is located in the taxonomy based on its procedural classification.

1.1.1.2. In-place destructive frozen nanobot replacement – This procedure is essentially the same as *destructive conscious nanobot replacement* (§1.1.1.1), except that the biological brain is frozen (static) during the procedure. Each nanobot still replaces an individually assigned neuron, thereby maintaining connectivity throughout a single brain. If one believes that neural function cannot be inferred from static structure, then that is a problem for all static procedures of course. Such a challenge might be resolved by modeling neural function via nondestructive scanning in advance of the actual frozen upload procedure. In such a two-step process, the nanobots would incorporate the noninvasively (or at least nondestructively) scanned functional behavior as well as connection structure when replacing a neuron. Note that any form of in-place nanobot replacement involves the same minimal spatial displacement of 5–100 microns per neural unit, which adds up to 500–10,000 km total. The notable question with regard to this scenario is whether we judge its success differently than §1.1.1.1, and if so, why.

1.1.1.2.1. Temporal discontinuity – It is worth noting that temporal continuity is essentially meaningless in any static scenario. We could replace the frozen neurons at various rates across a spectrum from gradual methods to global simultaneous replacement. How could these variations in replacement rate have any practical impact on our interpretation of the results? One might conclude that even if global simultaneous replacement is problematic for conscious replacement procedures, it is nevertheless tolerable for frozen replacement procedures.

1.1.1.2.2. Spatial discontinuity – Issues pertaining to spatial continuity become considerably more flexible in a frozen replacement scenario. At the low end, we have direct nanobot-to-neuron contact, where a nanobot resides adjacent to its assigned neuron, a distance shown to be 5–100 microns (§1.1.1.1). However, unlike conscious procedures, in which the need to maintain ongoing functionality likely limits the maximum distance (§1.1.1.1.2), we can seemingly extend this distance arbitrarily during a frozen procedure since there is no dynamic conscious continuity to preserve throughout the upload process. As presented so far, the procedure can produce a strange final product since the proposed nanobot displacement only moves the replaced cell somas with their nanobot counterparts but their synaptic connection points remain in their original locations. The resulting structure consists of nanobots at some distance, say on a nearby table, with long electrical or optical axons and dendrites extending several feet to the original table, which is now entirely devoid of biological matter *and* nanobots, but where the various synapses reside, which seems nonsensical. This oddity could be resolved if, when the second of a pair of connected nanobots replaces its neuron, the associated synapse is moved from the original biological location to wherever the nanobots are arranging themselves, say on another table.

1.1.1.2.3. **Frozen nondestructive brain-doubling** – §1.1.1.2.2 immediately lends itself to a further extrapolation. Perhaps the procedure does not need to be destructive. Please see §1.1.2.2.1 (*in-place nondestructive frozen brain-doubling with spatial discontinuity*) for a full description of this scenario. Most people would readily conclude that such a procedure has failed to successfully upload, although I prefer a different interpretation, as presented later.

1.1.2. **In-place nondestructive procedures** – These scenarios are rarely, if ever, given any consideration. I suspect they simply haven't occurred to very many people. Initially, they involve producing a computerized brain that resides in the skull alongside the biological brain without harming the original, although deeper scenarios in this section break that assumption.

1.1.2.1. **In-place nondestructive conscious nanobot brain-doubling** – This procedure is a variant on *gradual in-place replacement* (§1.1.1), in which the nanobots still model and replicate the behavior of their assigned neurons, but don't kill them. Furthermore, the nanobots *wire up* with one another fully isolated from the biological brain, so as to eventually construct a duplicate computerized brain sharing the same skull as the biological brain. The two brains receive identical sensory stimuli but otherwise remain functionally and behaviorally isolated. Crucially, the resulting computerized brain is materially identical to that in the more conventional scenarios presented under §1.1.1, and any analysis must bear that fact in mind. At first glance, this scenario may seem straightforward to interpret: aside from being wired into the same sensory stimuli, the two brains are otherwise no different from a scan-and-copy scenario (see §2) and we could thus assume that the original mind is untouched and that a duplicate mind (and its computerized brain) have come into being but have not *transferred* the mind. However, this scenario closely resembles the temporal-rate scenario previously presented (§1.1.1.1.1) as that scenario approaches the near-simultaneous global replacement end of the replacement-rate spectrum. In that scenario, the biological brain is destroyed almost simultaneously, and in this case, the biological brain survives, but in both cases a new computerized brain is instantiated almost instantaneously. Therefore, if we interpret §1.1.1.1.1 as a successful upload even at the nearly-simultaneous-replacement end of the spectrum (and if we don't accept it, then we are once again faced with choosing an arbitrary cutoff in replacement rate), then this brain-doubling scenario raises a serious challenge: if we grant the identity to the upload, in accordance with §1.1.1.1.1, then how can we deny that identity to the surviving biological original in this scenario, but if we grant it to the original in this scenario, then we are no longer compatible with §1.1.1.1.1. In later sections, I will present an alternative interpretation of this paradox.

1.1.2.1.1. Brain-doubling with temporary biological shutdown – In this variant, as each neuron is duplicated, its behavior is supplanted by the computerized replacement, just like a destructive nanobot procedure (§1.1.1.1), but in this case, nondestructively, with the biological neurons merely *turned off* instead of killed (the method of disabling a living neuron is unspecified, but could resemble any hypothetical quiescent state). Cognitive processing gradually shifts to the doubled computerized brain, just like §1.1.1.1, with the subject being conscious throughout the procedure, but the biological brain remains intact, albeit increasingly static (unconscious). So far, this scenario poses no new questions, the mind smoothly transfers to the new substrate and should be interpreted identically to §1.1.1.1—but we can now consider reawakening the dormant biological brain at a later time. Wakeful continual consciousness was maintained throughout a clearly gradual procedure, and has presumably *transferred* to the computerized brain (this presumption is required for consistency with §1.1.1.1), so how do we interpret the biological brain when we wake it up? Should we still consider the gradually consciously transferred upload to be *the* mind? If we would still assign the identity to the upload, then we must unbelievably deny that identity to the unharmed original biological brain, labeling it as the ostensible *duplicate*. Alternatively, if we would reassign the identity back to the original, then how does that conclusion impact the our interpretation of §1.1.1.1, which generally poses the least challenge of all conceivable scenarios to practically all readers? What if we simply don't reawaken the dormant original? Would we grant the identity to the upload or not? Crucially, how can any decision about the upload's ultimate status hinge on whether or not we awaken the unrelated biological brain? Our interpretation of the resulting computerized brain's mind should be identical under all these subtle variations, but what interpretation would be consistent in all cases? These issues pose a serious paradox, one which is addressed by the philosophy and theory presented in chapter four.

1.1.2.1.1.1. **Spatial translation** – It was demonstrated in §1.1.1.1.2 (*spectrum of spatial displacements*) that we could plausibly maintain conscious continuity over some range of spatial displacements between the neurons and their replacement nanobots. Such notions raise the possibility that the doubled brain could reside outside the original skull, consciously and gradually transferred throughout the procedure, yet leaving an unharmed, albeit unconscious, biological brain behind (the entire original person in effect)—which could then awaken at a later time. Take a moment to comprehend this scenario, for it poses one of the most serious paradoxes in mind-uploading interpretation. The subject lies down on operating table A. A new body (perhaps robotic, perhaps cloned) lies still on table B. Throughout the procedure the subject is awake and conscious. It is difficult to speculate on what their visual experience would be as their sense of location shifts, but once the procedure is completed, they would feel themselves on table B (or at some point prior to completion). Conscious continuity was preserved throughout the procedure. Furthermore, only a single cumulative brain was active at any moment; any given neuron was active in only one location at any given time, either in the original brain on table A or in the nanobot-formed brain on table B. The subject sits up on table B and looks at their original body on the other table, utterly dormant. But then the doctors reactivate the original brain and the person on table A sits up as well. Abstractly speaking, the analysis is not too different from §1.1.2.1.1, where this paradox was first posed, but comprehending it with an associated spatial translation, thereby leaving the original body and brain (an entire person) utterly unaltered, renders the paradox all the more bluntly. How should we interpret this scenario?

1.1.2.1.2. **In-place delayed destructive conscious nanobot replacement** – This scenario lies conceptually between §1.1.1.1 (fully destructive) and §1.1.2.1 (brain-doubling). We first perform §1.1.2.1, but at some later time (could be fractions of a second, could be years), the original biological brain is destroyed. The interpretation is relatively simple in fact. This scenario consists of killing a distinct mind and person and should be regarded as such. Some readers would make a bigger deal out of killing an original than an upload, while others would not. Some readers might find the procedure varyingly intolerable based on the duration of the delay, while some may see no relevance in such distinctions. This scenario is included in the taxonomy because, despite its apparent absurdity, variations on it (usually not honoring the in-place component and usually presented in a scan-and-copy fashion, §2.2.1.1 notably) crop up in debates with remarkable regularity.

1.1.2.2. **In-place nondestructive frozen brain-doubling** – This procedure would be quite similar to the conscious variant (§1.1.2.1). The only difference would be that the mind is static and unconscious during the procedure. After completion, both resulting brains would wake up and proceed as in the conscious scenario. This procedure is also very similar to brain-doubling with temporary shutdown (§1.1.2.1.1) except that it doesn't involve conscious dynamic smooth transfer of function since the brain is frozen during the procedure.

1.1.2.2.1. **Spatial discontinuity** – §1.1.2.2 (*in-place nondestructive frozen brain-doubling*) can be extended to support spatial translations in the same way I have described for other procedures. Thus, we could produce an upload at *next-table* distance, while leaving the frozen original unharmed. Most people would reject such a procedure, judging it a failure to *transfer* the mind, since the original is unharmed and potentially revivable, although I present an alternative interpretation later.

1.2. **Non-in-place procedures** – At first glance, one might assume that replacement procedures (much less, gradual replacement procedures) must, by their very nature, be in-place, resulting in a computerized brain in the same skull as that of the biological brain. In earlier sections of the taxonomy, some extrapolations stretched and effectively broke this assumption. However, ironically, one of the oldest formally described procedures violates this expectation out of the box.

1.2.1. **Moravec bush-robot** – This procedure was originally described by Hans Moravec [31, 32]. It involves a robot with a set of tree-branch-like fractal appendages that fork repeatedly from a macroscopic root (where the robot is literally rooted to the operating table) to final digits of cellular or sub-cellular scale (see figure 1). The robot settles this *bush*, as he called it, onto the outer surface of the exposed biological brain, which may be conscious throughout the procedure. The robot's billions of microscopic terminal digits impinge upon the brain at an appropriate spacing (perhaps microns). These terminal digits then scan the neural structure and function immediately within reach. This thin outer layer of neural structure is then replicated via a second bush appendage (attached to the same root, the robot has two primary arms) on a second table. Neural connectivity is maintained between the biological brain and the incomplete computerized brain throughout the procedure via the internal branches of the robot. With the outer layer of the brain scanned and duplicated, it is then vaporized and the bush descends a microscopic distance into the skull cavity. This process continues such that half-way through the procedure the top-half of the biological brain is gone and the bottom half of the computerized brain is not yet built. Singular conscious identity is maintained throughout the procedure exactly as in a nanobot in-place procedure. There is but a single, fully connected brain at all times, which should satisfy the requirements of even the most conservative gradual replacement enthusiasts. As the procedure concludes, the skull is fully scooped out like a jack-o'-lantern, with the bush reaching right to the bottom (or deeper into the central nervous system, as the reader may require), and the computerized brain is then complete and can operate on its own without the bush robot scaffolding. Should we consider this to be a spatially continuous upload, despite producing a computerized brain that resides at next-table distance from the biological brain?

1.2.1.1. Nondestructive bush-robot with temporary biological shutdown – This procedure is essentially §1.1.2.1.1.1 (*brain-doubling with temporary shutdown with spatial translation*). Please see elsewhere in the taxonomy.

1.2.1.2. Multi-armed bush-robot – In this variant, the bush robot has three arms. One scans and destroys the biological brain and two others build two brains on two nearby operating tables. It is unclear how they would maintain functionality, how they would share *control* between their now duplicated corresponding features (there were no duplicated features in the former scenario; a given neuron existed either in the biological brain of the computerized brain, but never both). Nevertheless, this scenario is tantalizing.

~ ~ ~

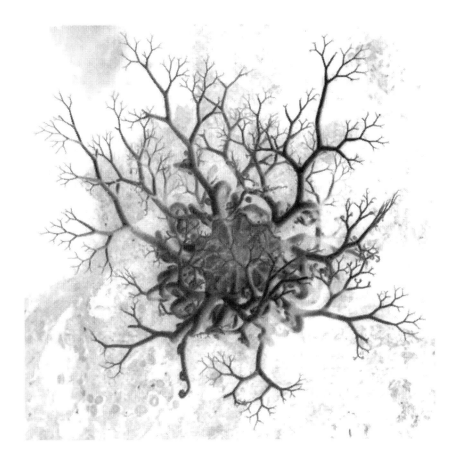

Figure 1. Gorgonocephalus eucnemis (basket star) – The Basket Star (a type of brittle star, which is closely related to starfish) was recognized by Moravec as a living organism that closely reflects the basic design and intent of a fractal bush robot [32]. Many impressive examples can easily be found online.

2. SCAN-AND-DUPLICATE PROCEDURES – Unlike in-place replacement procedures, scan-and-duplicate procedures can more readily produce not only physical brains, but also virtual brains (simulations), and can more readily accommodate abstractions of neural function (described as higher-order brains in the glossary).

2.1. Frozen scan-and-copy procedures – Procedures in which the biological brain is frozen and static during the scanning process. Notice that unlike conscious procedures, listed below (§2.2), no taxonomic distinction is made between instantaneous and noninstantaneous scans. Frozen brains are, by definition, nontemporal entities, and as such, temporal properties, such as scan-rate, do not apply, i.e., no meaningful changes in interpretation can be justified on the basis of varying scan-rates so all scan-rates are interpretatively identical.

2.1.1. Frozen destructive scan-and-copy – This scenario bears the distinction of being the closest to a plausible technology in the entire taxonomy, the most likely to first become truly realizable as technology evolves. In fact, preliminary aspects of this process are already operational technologies today. Both mouse and human brains have been scanned, and their connectomes inferred to varying degrees of precision, using this method [1, 35]. The basic approach consists of slicing the entire three-dimensional frozen brain into numerous two-dimensional sections, scanning the two-dimensional sections, deducing the three-dimensional structure (the connectome), and then rebuilding that structure in a three-dimensional simulation or emulation (a virtual structural brain in the glossary). What remains to bring such a technology to full mind-uploading is to increase the resolution and overall quality of the scan, and then develop software simulations of the reconstructed network structure, along with the required computational hardware to run such simulations at real-time speed (these challenges are not to be taken lightly; we have a long way to go yet). More fundamentally, it remains to be seen to what extent a mere connectome (mere structural knowledge), with no direct scanning of online neural function, and no scanning of the dynamic chemical environment of the brain, can actually replicate the mind. This is simply an open question at the current time (I admit to being sympathetic to the concern myself). If a purely static scan is insufficient to the ultimate goals of mind-uploading, then conscious scanning, for the purpose of deducing per-neuron functional behavior, may be required. This claim presents a serious challenge to all static methods (although they may be augmented as a hybrid procedure which combines online scan information from prior to the upload procedure with the latter upload procedure itself). Various targets are listed under *brain* in the glossary and shown in figure 2. They are as follows in the next subsections.

2.1.1.1. **Physical biological brain (a clone)** – Historically, this procedure has not been described as mind-uploading, which is usually preserved for computers, androids, etc., but rather as a form of cloning, in which a second normal biological human is produced. This method should not be confused with the modern scientific process of cloning, the crucial difference between the fictional and scientific uses of the term being the status of the brain and mind. In the former, the brain is assumed to be perfectly cloned as well, thereby producing a duplicated brain (whether the mind, the *person*, is regarded as duplicated is a deeper philosophical question, explored later). In the latter, what is cloned is merely the genome of an organism, but not its neurological brain structure or associated mental phenomena.

2.1.1.2. **Physical computerized brain** – This procedure produces a computerized structure that operates much like the brain. It ostensibly consists of billions of independent computer processors arranged into a physical network whose topology reflects the scanned biological brain toward the goal of replicating the functional and behavioral methods employed by the original brain. This is the sort of brain generally produced by gradual replacement procedures (see §1).

2.1.1.3. **Virtual structural brain (spatial emulation)** – This procedure produces a mind that runs within a software emulation of the spatial arrangement of parts comprising the original biological brain. The actual computation does not rely on a physically analogous network of processors, but rather builds and operates a three-dimensional physical emulation of a brain, including all required spatial coordinates, relationships, gradients, etc. In theory, such an emulation might run on a computer not too unlike contemporary computers, although it is questionable whether such devices could ever offer the necessary performance to run such an emulation at real-time speeds. Massively parallel computers will probably be required.

2.1.1.4. Virtual functional brain (behavioral emulation) – This procedure produces a mind that dispenses with the spatial arrangement of parts that make up a brain and merely emulates the abstract network topology of the brain. This is how most historical and modern neural network systems operate. As in the case of a spatially emulated brain, the actual hardware running the emulation might be relatively similar to contemporary computers, with the previously stated caveat as to requisite performance.

2.1.1.5. Virtual higher-order brain (abstracted behavioral emulation) – This procedure builds and runs an emulation of high-level cognitive processes or algorithms that, in concert, give rise to the intellect of a mind. In the biological case, these cognitive functions are encoded in lower-order neural structures, but once we understand how neural structures give rise to cognitive functionality, we may simply modularize such neural structures as algorithmic *black boxes*. Some people would certainly reject such an upload as not capturing the original mind, and possibly as not even housing a conscious fully realized human mind. Examples of such modular groupings might include receptive fields, cortical columns, or possibly entire brain regions, like the hippocampus, where some progress has already been made [19].

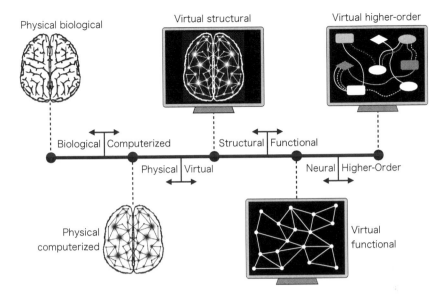

Figure 2. Brain categories – This figure shows one possible categorization of brain types. They are described in the glossary under *brain* and in the taxonomy in §2.1.1.1–2.1.1.5. The five types can be arranged along a spectrum of functional abstraction as described in the glossary under *substrate* (see table 1) and here:

- *Biological vs. computerized* – Biological brains are comprised of biological components, e.g., neurons. Computerized brains are artificial (they use computerized hardware and either computerized or virtual components).

- *Physical vs. virtual* – Physical brains involve real physical network structure, either neural or computerized. Virtual brains run on simulations and emulations.

- *Structural vs. functional* – Structural brains consist of a spatial network of neural units, and include spatial network simulations. Functional brains are nonspatially organized (they only replicate network topology).

- *Neural vs. higher-order* – Neural brains operate at the level of networked neurons, whether physical, spatial, or even merely conceptual (virtual functional). Higher-order brains, operate at a level of computational abstraction considerably higher than neural units, e.g., computational modules that perform compartmentalized operations (see §2.1.1.5).

2.1.2. Frozen nondestructive scan-and-copy – From the POV of the upload, this procedure *feels* identical to a destructive procedure (§2.1.1); the uploaded mind can't determine which procedure occurred based on the information or experience available. However, this procedure permits the original brain and mind to awaken after the procedure, which has dramatic implications on assignment of identity. There are three scenarios worth considering:

2.1.2.1. Both brains are awakened in naturally varying sensory environments – (perhaps on different operating tables, in different rooms, or perhaps on different planets or separated in time by thousands of years!). Their brain-states and mind-states (see philosophical discussion later, notably chapter five) should instantaneously diverge, thus yielding two (or more) unique and fully personified individuals from the instant they awaken. Whether to interpret this scenario as a successful or failed upload is a deep philosophical question about which people often strongly disagree. This book presents a relatively novel philosophy and interpretation later.

2.1.2.2. Both brains are awakened in essentially identical sensory environments – They then remain in these identical environments for an *experimentally interesting* duration of time. Their brain-states and mind-states will metaphysically diverge instantaneously, thus granting each the full rights of any individual person, but they might *meaningfully* diverge rather slowly. They may appear rather similar both in external behavior and in internal mental-state for quite a *long time*, whatever duration that phrase implies. It is an open question how rapidly they would achieve various potential milestones of divergence.

2.1.2.3. Both brains are awakened in identical sensory environments in a deterministic universe: The White Room – Both brains are awakened in, and remain forever in, identical sensory environments in a hypothetical deterministic universe. Please see the section entitled *The White Room* for a thorough analysis of this scenario.

2.2. **Conscious scan-and-copy procedures** – Procedures in which the biological brain is conscious and awake during the scanning process.

2.2.1. **Conscious destructive** – Procedures in which the biological brain is destroyed during the scanning process, but in which the experience of conscious continuity is preserved:

2.2.1.1. **Conscious destructive scan-and-copy with instantaneous scan: Teleportation** – This scenario closely resembles the intent, if not necessarily the concept, of *teleportation*, the best distinction probably being that some definitions of teleportation might require sending (spatially translating) the actual physical matter of the teleporting object to the new location as opposed to merely sending its structural pattern description. Definitions of teleportation that would accommodate merely transmitting and reconstructing the material pattern are indistinguishable from this uploading scenario. There is frequent debate over the identity of the upload and/or the death of the original in various scenarios of this type. The acceptance of shows like Star Trek, with its teleporting *transporter*, inspires confidence, but the debate rages on. Up-and-coming technologies will continue to test the boundaries of our philosophical interpretation of these scenarios as nascent 3D scanners and printers gain capability. We will first apply such questions to static material objects, i.e., does a scanner/transmitter/printer *teleport* a plastic cup, or merely duplicate it? Instead of reflexively preferring one answer over the other, I encourage the reader to consider the issue with an open and uncommitted mind, for the question is far more interesting than the answer. As the technology further evolves, we will have to contend with increasingly dynamic material objects, then plant-like biological systems, and eventually simple animals. Ultimately, the combined evolving technologies of scanning, data-transmission, and printing (building) may force us to contend with full-blown uploading or human-teleportation implications.

2.2.1.2. Conscious destructive scan-and-copy with noninstantaneous scan – This is a pretty inconceivable procedure since the remaining portion of the biological brain midway through the scan would lack the destroyed part of the brain with which to interact. It is included to complete the taxonomy but a feasible procedure is not easily imagined.

2.2.2. Conscious nondestructive – Procedures in which the biological brain is conscious and need not be destroyed by the scanning process. Early generation technologies include MRI, MEG, etc. The spirit of the scenarios in this section extends these nascent technologies to hypothetical methods that would enable scans of sufficient spatial and temporal precision to enable mind-uploading.

2.2.2.1. Conscious nondestructive scan-and-copy with instantaneous scan – Synonymous with a §2.1.1 (*frozen nondestructive scan*) except without an unconscious break in cognition. The original biological brain and mind's POV is that the procedure has not occurred (which is generally true of conscious procedures). Note that the duplication process need not necessarily be instantaneous, in which case the upload may begin running with a state lagging in time behind the original, namely the state at the time of the scan. We can consider the following variants:

2.2.2.1.1. Nonidentical setting for the upload's reception – The upload's POV is of instantly teleporting without *sleeping-and-awakening* (his visual surroundings and conscious experience suddenly flash to a new setting). Note that from the upload's POV, this scenario is indistinguishable from destructive teleportation (§2.2.1.1).

2.2.2.1.2. Identical setting with respect to sensory input – The upload's POV is identical to that of the original, namely that the procedure has not occurred. The various subtleties of this scenario are explored under *frozen nondestructive scan-and-copy* (§2.1.2). The only difference from §2.1.2 is that neither mind experiences unconsciousness (sleep) during the procedure.

2.2.2.2. Conscious nondestructive scan-and-copy with noninstantaneous scan – The upload will begin from a state lagging behind the original. More seriously the upload's initial state will be a conscious temporal blur with earlier scanned portions correspond to older brain state. Would the uploaded brain naturally accommodate this error and continue unharmed, or is this a fundamental inconsistency with this procedure? Alternatively, the duplication may occur online with the scan, which could resolve the temporal inconsistency as well as the temporal lag. Nevertheless, this scenario poses significant challenges to interpretation of the upload's *experience* during the procedure; it is unclear what this procedure would feel like to the upload.

$$\sim \ \sim \ \sim$$

3. **BRAIN DIVISION SCENARIOS** – These scenarios are highly analogous to cell division. Brain division and reconstruction involve an initial nondestructive scan of the entire brain, followed by division and then duplication or cloning of some number of *portions* of the brain, followed by reconstruction of multiple complete brains, each containing some original biological structure and some new computerized structure (see figure 3). If full computerization is required of a complete uploading procedure, then a necessary second step would involve computerizing the remaining biological structure, perhaps via §1.1.1.1 since most people consider it the most palatable scenario of all.

These scenarios specifically investigate the issue of identity with respect to material continuity (i.e., the importance of preserving original brain matter in identifying the resulting minds). As will be shown in the subscenarios, some derivations converge on scenarios described elsewhere in the taxonomy. For simplicity, these procedures may be regarded as frozen unconscious: any resulting minds, original, upload, or otherwise, have the POV of *going to sleep* before the procedure and *waking up* afterwards. Potential implications of conscious versions of these scenarios are not considered here, but should readily be extrapolated from the available taxonomy.

An important point to bear in mind when judging or interpreting division scenarios is that even from the internal subjective perspective of the various resulting minds, there is no way to tell who is who. That is to say that if *you* are one of the minds resulting from, say, §3.2 below, you have no idea whether your brain contains 99% or 1% original biological brain. In fact, no one else can tell either, short of peeking inside your skull, and even then they can only tell the difference on the assumption that the upload substrate can actually be discerned from the original substrate (which could be next to impossible in a biological cloning scenario as opposed to a computerized scenario).

Note that this divide-and-reconstruct method is, in effect, synonymous with the *discrete neuron-batch* interpretation of *gradual nanobot in-place replacement* (§1.1.1.1.1.2). If we accept the batch-based approach as a successful upload, we must accept the divide-and-reconstruct procedure at equivalent batch scales. The only difference is that the divide-and-reconstruct procedure leaves us pondering the status of the additional reconstructed brains.

3.1. **Divide brain at 50%** – Divide the brain into two halves. Clone (or computerize) each half. Rebuild two brains (either fully biological or partly biological and partly computerized) with equal portions of the original biological brain. Questions: What happened to the original mind? *Where* is it? From *where* did a second mind arise? How do we assign various identities to the resulting minds? Who gets to claim primacy of the original identity? Lest the reader feel any temptation to interpret the two brains' primacy to the original differently on the basis that the left and right hemispheres are well established to serve heterogenous roles in cognition, realize that sagittal-division (left/right division, as shown in figure 3, subfigure A) is merely a simplification of the concept; division could be evenly distributed throughout the brain (see figure 3, subfigure B).

3.2. **Divide at 1%** – Divide at approximately one billion neurons. Clone two missing pieces. Rebuild two brains. Let us consider the 99% biological brain with 1% replacement. Does it house the original mind given that it contains 99% of the original brain? If so, and if per chance the 50% scenario was rejected as not preserving the mind, then what is the dividing point at which we consider the larger biological portion to have maintained the original mind? Is this dividing point arbitrary or rationally justified?

3.3. **Divide at 51%** – Clone and rebuild two brains. Similar questions apply. If we accepted 99% but rejected 50%, then there must be some cutoff in between. What about 51%? 67%? More importantly, can we justify our choice of cutoff rationally and objectively? Additionally, what status do we assign to the brain with the smaller original portion? Before proceeding, briefly consider a 67%/33% division in greater detail. Should we accept the 33% brain as a legitimate upload?

3.4. **Divide at 33% 3 times** – Produce three brains, each with 33% biological brain. Curiously, if when choosing a cutoff in §3.3, the reader accepted a cutoff below 33%, this immediately implies tolerance of a three-way split (see figure 3, subfigure E), thereby proposing the possibility of multi-uploading.

3.5. **Divide at 1% 100 times** – Produce 100 brains, each containing 1% of the original. All parts are equally original, as in §3.4. What are we to make of this potential bulk uploading scenario?

3.6. **Divide at 1/100-billionth** – This is one end of the spectrum of possibilities (with 50% being the other end). In this case, a single neuron is the dividing point. With respect to the larger portion, this scenario is synonymous with the first step in §1.1.1.1 (*gradual in-place nanobot replacement*), and thus is generally assumed (by those who view mind-uploading favorably in the first place) to house the original mind (in fact, we *must* hold this view since brains lose individual neurons relatively frequently and we happily consider such loss to be ineffective upon identity). But what then of the other brain (housing a single biological neuron) and its mind?

3.7. **Divide at 1/100-billionth 100 billion times** – This is the limit of the brain division scenarios, analogous to §3.1 (two resulting brains), §3.4 (three brains), and §3.5 (100 brains), in which all resulting brains contain equal parts of the original brain. In this case, we produce 100 billion brains, each housing a single neuron from the original brain. Should we judge this scenario any differently than the others?

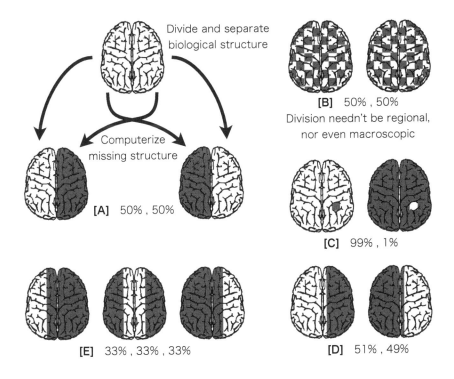

Divide and separate biological structure

Computerize missing structure

[A] 50% , 50%

[B] 50% , 50%
Division needn't be regional, nor even macroscopic

[C] 99% , 1%

[E] 33% , 33% , 33%

[D] 51% , 49%

Figure 3. Brain division – This figure shows several brain division scenarios, wherein some portion of the original biological brain is preserved in the resulting brains. Ostensibly, the upload process could be completed in a second step that computerizes the remaining biological structure via §1.1.1.1. The simplest example is a 50% split [A]. If the reader is tempted to assign unequal primacy on the basis that the two halves are definitively heterogenous in function and role, realize that the illustration is merely conceptual and can be extended in sophistication [B]. After contemplating the interpretation of a 50% split, next consider a 99%/1% split [C]. If the interpretations accept 50% but reject 1% then consider 51%/49% [D]? Ultimately, what is the reader's tolerance cutoff and how is that cutoff justified? Lastly, observe that division can readily produce numerous equivalent brains and minds [E]. If the reader would assign a cutoff that accepts 67%/33% in a two-way split (not shown), then what would that imply for a three split as shown?

•

Section 2

•

~ *4* ~

Metaphysics

Chapters two and three presented a glossary and a taxonomy. In those chapters, I attempted to minimize the exposition of my personal beliefs or philosophy, that is, to define terms for the rest of the book and to survey hypothetical scenarios (thought experiments) without recommending too many conclusions or interpretations of those experiments. Admittedly, such intentions are only partially satisfied and both the glossary and taxonomy are surely laced with the undercurrents of my pervading views; nevertheless, I strived thusly. In the remaining chapters, I present my personal brand of philosophy on these topics and argue them to the best of my (current) ability.

Motive

I am troubled by what I perceive as a cultural bias favoring or dismissing various subjective perspectives in the kinds of thought experiments mind-uploading inspires, and more precisely, in pondering the uploading question. As per the glossary, by subjective perspective I refer to the POV, feelings, self-interpretation, and sense-of-identity of a given mind. Although that description is rather vague, it really just boils down to your individual sense of who you are as a person and how you are consciously unique from other people.

A common reaction to, or interpretation of, the mind-uploading scenarios presented in the taxonomy is that we can qualitatively judge the results (i.e., deem the procedure a success or a failure) by inquiring the POV of one of the minds with disregard (or less regard) to the POV of the others. Virtually without exception, such a bias favors the original biological brain and its mind, and dismisses the upload's brain and its mind (or multiple uploads and their minds). There is a three-tiered situation involved here:

1. *Bias* (the holding of an unbalanced view favoring one thing over another), which can readily lead to...
2. *Prejudice* (the subsequent position that bias underlies a genuine and justified difference in substantial value, i.e., the assignment of superiority, primacy, or validity to one at the expense of another), which can lead to...
3. *Discrimination* (actions favoring the well-being, liberty, happiness, and even life of some while dismissing, subjugating, or even disregarding the life of others).

In the realm of thought experiment, and so long as these technologies are not yet remotely feasible, the risks of bias, prejudice and discrimination are not too serious—but one day we may conceivably face these or related issues under more plausible and consequently more serious circumstances. I foresee a likely risk that we could not only denigrate the self-professed POV of uploads (which would, at worst, insult them), but more seriously, that we may also denigrate their rights, and quite possibly their lives. As we attempt to refrain from taking all of this hypothetical pondering too seriously (I may have already failed in that regard), we should nevertheless bear in the mind the possibility that this topic could evolve into something more pressing and societally relevant—some day.

Toward the aim of alleviating the risks of bias and related circumstances, I argue for an extremely centrist interpretation, distributing primacy of post-upload minds relative to their claim to the original mind with essentially uncompromising equality. Although that claim is formally stated in chapter seven, I urge the reader to advance methodically, for the weight of the conclusion is only bolstered by the full exposition leading up to it. That is, in a sense, the entire purpose of this book. Merely stating my final conclusion (my position of equality of various minds across a wide range of uploading scenarios) would not require a book, nor even a lengthy paper. Paragraphs would suffice for the task. My goal in writing this book is to present an end-to-end argument that leads up to, and essentially derives, that final conclusion practically ipso facto.

Disclaimer (about language)

Our language does not lend itself well to these kinds of discussions. We use words like *original*, *copy*, *duplicate*, *clone*, etc., generally ignoring the fact that they presuppose obvious values: being original is a superior state while being a copy is woefully denigrated by comparison. Such language precludes any attempt to debate these issues on level ground as the bias intrinsic to these words undermines our objectivity before the discussion begins. Without better options, I myself resort to these words on occasion, but bear in mind that I use them solely to indicate which brain or mind is which in the scenario, but not to assign any presumed value whatsoever.

Our problems with language don't end there. A common assumption is that a mind is a singular thing and may be described in singular terms. We speak of *a* mind or *the* mind. Likewise, when we speak of *transferring* a mind we are considering how it is located in space and how it can move from one spatial location to another (notionally from one brain to another, either of which might be physical or virtual). Other terms related to mind presume similar singularness: *I*, *me*, *you*, *him/her*, etc. These words imply (and prescribe) assumptions about the nature, boundaries, and properties of identity, as well as the sorts of transformations that can be performed on identity. The theory presented below violates many common instincts which are presupposed by such language, yet our language is the one with which I must communicate, so I will muddle through as best as possible and endeavor to explain when and where my theory departs from the innate assumptions of the language with which it is conveyed.

Metaphysics

Before we can consider topics as specific as brains and minds, we must establish a foundation, starting with what philosophers call metaphysics. This is the branch of philosophy that is perhaps the most fundamental yet vaguest of them all. It directly involves concepts as confusing and nondescript as the nature of reality, the properties and qualities of existence—that sort of fluff. Yet, despite its flirtation with pointlessness, I resistantly find it crucial to consider these topics carefully.

I came to metaphysics reluctantly. When I began this book, my intent was simply to lay out the arguments for my view of the relationship between brains and minds, and the implications of that view on the possible transformations to minds, namely mind-uploading. However I found that I could not clearly describe these ideas without delving into metaphysics, first a short distance, then further still as I attempted to clarify the concepts on which my exposition would rest. Yet, I still strive to confine metaphysical navel-gazing to the barest minimum required in order to firmly establish the topics that are of more direct interest: minds and mind-uploading. Since metaphysical philosophy can get pretty abstruse, I confine my introduction to the few specific topics most salient to minds. These topics are universals, particulars, types, tokens, and occurrences. Admittedly, each of these terms is subject to debate among both ancient and contemporary philosophers, so all I can offer is my personal interpretation. Where the reader disagrees with me, I must ask that he or she indulge my eccentricities or else show themselves the exit as so they may choose.

Universals, Realism, Tokens, Occurrences

With that disclaimer out of the way, universals are abstract qualities of one of three kinds: types (multi-item groupings of shared identity, e.g., roses, thorns, leaves), properties (single-item qualities, e.g., redness[6], sharpness, flatness), and relations (two-item inequalities, e.g., redder, sharper, flatter) [49]. Platonic realism (clearly originating with the great Plato himself) claims that these concepts exist in their own right in some nonspatio-temporal domain, and that physical objects may exhibit or qualify them (I like to refer to this concept as embedding or instantiating a universal). Aristotelian realism, on the other hand (Aristotle being Plato's student if the reader is unaware), claims that universals only exist once they are instantiated by particulars (e.g., an actual rose instantiates and *brings into being* the rose type or the red property). In addition to the Platonic and Aristotelian perspectives, there are a few variations. Notably, nominalists go so far as to deny universals entirely, while conceptualists permit universals to exist, but only as perceived by a conscious mind to recognize and label them. I prefer the Platonic approach, that universals exist independent of any association, requiring neither physical instance nor conscious recognition in order to exist. I believe the notions of *circle* (a type universal) and of *circularity* (a property universal) exist even if no circles actually exist. For example, until the very moment that this sentence was first conceived in my mind, no one had ever before considered the polygon with 2304982039 sides, but I claim that it existed no less than the square, despite our having overlooked it until now (see figure 4). To my understanding, an Aristotelian, a nominalist, and a conceptualist would all disagree with such a position.

---

[6] Both Chalmers and Dennett insightfully show that color may be a rather poor example of a well-defined *type*, in so far as its qualification depends to a significant extent on labeling by a conscious perceiver as opposed to being intrinsic to physical objects (in this way it conforms more closely to *conceptualism* than Platonism or Aristotelianism, described in this same section), but I maintain color's use as a example due to its near-ubiquity in such philosophical explorations [8, 13].

Figure 4. Platonic vs. Aristotelian type invocation – I must have drawn hundreds, if not thousands, of these elaborate shapes in the margins of my notebooks in high school and college. Over time, I developed a set of rules that governed how to properly generate *legal* shapes in this style so as to produce infinite variety, yet semi-structured consistency. A Platonist would say I *discovered* each shape from within a space of all possible shapes conforming to the prescribed rules, while an Aristotelian would say I *created* each one. Not only do I feel Platonic about the shapes themselves, but to an even greater extent, I feel particularly Platonic about the rules that generate and restrict them; I feel that over time I *discovered* the rules for generating these shapes, as opposed to feeling like I created those rules[7]—and yes, I sold some as *flash* to tattoo parlors, including custom designing a large pattern in this style for a friend.

---

[7] A related anecdote tells the story of how Douglas Crockford claims not to have invented JSON, but rather to have *discovered* it: "*I discovered JSON. I do not claim to have invented JSON because it already existed in nature. What I did was I found it, I named it, I described how it was useful.*" [10]. This is a highly Platonic perspective.

With universals, and specifically type universals, now briefly defined, we can consider another metaphysical concept: tokens, actual spatio-temporal (i.e., material) instances of universals. An actual physical dish is a token of the following universal kinds: a *type* of dining paraphernalia that exhibits the *property* of circularity and exhibits the *relation* of larger-than relative to the saucer token.

However, instantiated types don't have to be tokens, that is to say, they don't have to be spatio-temporal. Nonspatio-temporal type instantiations are called abstract particulars or abstract occurrences (with tokens being concrete occurrences). A common example of an abstract particular is numbers [16], which are discussed in greater detail below. Note that types can easily be hierarchical (planets, which are a type of astronomical body, are also *types of spheres*, where spheres are clearly types of geometrical forms themselves).

Given tokens as physical occurrences, and abstract occurrences as nonphysical occurrences, we can then simply refer to occurrences, which indicate any and all instantiations of a type. Occurrences can be either abstract or physical, and are called abstract occurrences and tokens respectively.

The most common example used to discriminate the three concepts of type, occurrence, and token is the exemplary sentence, *"A rose is a rose is a rose is a rose"*[8] (or variations that appear in the literature) [45, 49]. The sentence itself is a type (namely, a specific type of sentence amongst all possible sentences). The sentence can be embedded physically (e.g., with ink on paper or light on a screen), in which case we have a token of the corresponding sentence type. However, we can also conceive of the sentence without necessarily giving it physical form. For example, we may say that the sentence is part of a larger textual work, such as the poem from which it originates. We can hold an instance of the sentence in our minds, as you are doing right now. In

---

[8] It is common for some culturally idiosyncratic examplar to be latched upon by an intellectual inner-circle. A famous example is the Lena photo used throughout the computer science community for image-processing experiments (all the more salacious for the photo having originated as a Playboy centerfold no less) [6]. In this case, Gertrude Stein's poem *Sacred Emily* gives us the line *"A rose is a rose is a rose is a rose."*, which metaphysical discussions concerning types and occurrences have similarly adopted [45, 49].

these forms it is an abstract occurrence: it is instantiated, but not spatio-temporally as physical matter.

Likewise, much as the sentence may conceptually occur within a poem, we may consider the words comprising the sentence, which when written down, become tokens of their respective word types. In physical form, there are clearly eleven word tokens in the written sentence. However, in its abstract (nonspatio-temporal) occurrence, the sentence definitively cannot be composed of tokens, for tokens are physical. So what are we to make of the eleven things that make up the abstract occurrence of the sentence, the notion of the sentence? These things are abstract occurrences of three possible word types (*a*, *rose* and *is*). Likewise, as stated, the entire sentence may be an abstract occurrence within some larger text. So, the abstract form of the sentence (the nonspatio-temporal version not given physical form) contains eleven word occurrences which instantiate one of three word types, all without resorting to physical reality at all. Remarkably, the summary of this paragraph will be relevant to the later discussion.

One point worth emphasizing is that types cannot be composed of other types, but rather of abstract occurrences. One reason is that types can never exist twice, but components can exist twice within a type, so those components can't possibly be other types. Consider the *moon* word type. It is composed of some *letter* entities, four of them in fact. These four entities cannot be types, because the '*o*' entity is represented twice, which types can't do: '*o*' as a concept only exists once. Therefore, we say that the *moon* word type is composed of four letter occurrences, each instantiating one of three letter types: '*m*', '*o*', and '*n*'. This example illustrates why we need a third concept between types and tokens, the abstract occurrence. Entities such as the two letter '*o*'s in the word *moon* cannot be tokens, but also cannot be types, so they are this other concept, nonspatio-temporal occurrences, or simply abstract occurrences (remember, occurrences that aren't abstract are implicitly spatio-temporal, i.e., simply tokens).

Numerals

Numbers are the focus of my considerations below (namely, *information* as Claude Shannon presented the notion), so I will focus on them. Numbers can be described in the following fashion. The digits defining a given numerical base are digit types (we work with ten of these digit types in our more comfortable base). The base itself is also a type, that of a positional numerical-representation. Sequences of digits equate to what we call numerals and are also types (each unique sequence being a type of digit sequence). One might assume that unique digit sequences aren't types, but rather are actual instances of numerals (occurrences of some sort). This isn't correct. Much like the *rose is a rose* sentence, which was merely a sentence type *awaiting* instantiation, a specific digit sequence is just a type of numeral. It may help to realize that a specific digit sequence can only conceptually exist once, which is one of the traits of a type, not an occurrence.

Given a specific numeral type, say 123, we can instantiate it, as we are doing right now in our thoughts and as it is intrinsically instantiated in this very sentence. Furthermore, if we write that numeral down on paper (or as you are currently viewing it here), we may now refer to a numeral token of the 123 type, i.e., a spatio-temporal occurrence composed of individual spatio-temporal digit tokens: '1', '2', and '3'. Figure 5 offers some insight into numeral tokenization.

One thing to keep clear is the distinction between length-one digit sequences (i.e., numerals) and digits (the types from which numerals are constructed). They are not the same thing. The numeral '5' (what we could colloquially call the *number* five or use as a value to label a count of five apples on a table) is actually a numeral, a digit sequence composed of one occurrence of the '5' digit type. This concept is pretty strange and vague at first glance. It is similar to the difference between the letter '*a*' and the word "*a*".

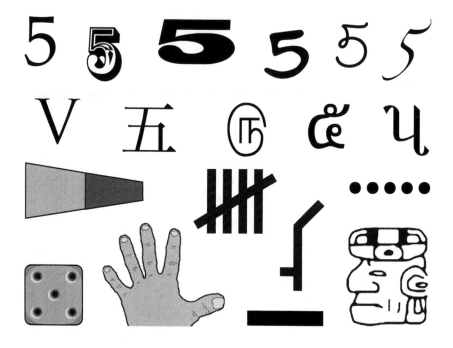

Figure 5. A sample of '5'-numeral-type tokens – This figure shows a sample of the infinite variety of tokens that embed or instantiate the '5' numeral type. Not only are there a truly infinite number of subtle variations on Arabic script, as shown along the top row (all examples of tokens that embed the Arabic '5' character type to represent the '5' digit type within the '5' numeral type—*whoa!*), but there are numerous nonArabic scripts, as shown in the second row (Roman, Chinese, Tamil, Thai, Gujarati), as well as abstract tokens not associated with a language, shown on the bottom (nautical flag, hashes, semaphore, quincunx dice, fingers). The last three tokens, at lower-right, are actually linguistic again, like those in the top two rows: five dots indicate a Morse code '5' (although also simply indicate a general unary-base representation) while a single rectangular bar or a face with a *Tun* glyph over it are both Mayan forms.

It can help to keep track of is which entities can instantiate multiple times at any given level of abstraction. The sentence type *"A rose is a rose is a rose is a rose"* contains multiple occurrences of various word types, but there is only one word type representing *rose*. Likewise, a numeral may contain multiple occurrences of a given digit type. For example, 34534 is a numeral type containing two abstract occurrences of the '3' and '4' digit types. In a physical tokenized form of the numeral (ink on paper), it would contain two tokens of each of the '3' and '4' digit types as well. While the occurrences of the digits are distinct (that is to say the digits occur multiple times), those digit occurrences nevertheless refer to a single shared type, the '3' or '4' digit type respectively. That realization is, of course, what ties the multiple 3s together, the fact that they really truly do refer to a single shared concept, the underlying type. This commonality that gives the multiple occurrences of '3' a shared identity *is* the type, literally by definition.

The subtlest concept is the overall numeral itself, aka, the entire sequence of digits. Why can't we say that the 34534 type exists multiple times, other than by definition, which feels logically circular? It helps to disambiguate the type from its occurrences. 34534, as a type, indicates a unique notion of a numeral, the *idea* of that particular numeral, not just some instance of it. It simply doesn't make sense to suggest that an identical grouping may exist, *as a unique way of grouping digits*, multiple times. The concept of grouping digits in just that way, and no other way, can only be such a concept once. To follow through, just as the '3' digit type and the '3' numeral type both occur in the 34534 numeral type multiple times, we may say that the 34 numeral type also occurs in 34534, and occurs multiple times at that.

All that said, there is a theory call the Prefix Proposal which suggests that occurrences are actually also unique, much like types, with their uniqueness deriving from their precise position in a sequence, and therefore that they don't represent multi-occurrences either, but rather represent single occurrences of unique types [49]. Two seemingly similar occurrences are then disambiguated by taking into account their overall position in a sequence. However, I am unconvinced by this theory and will not consider it further here. I prefer the interpretation I have presented, that occurrences can truly multi-instantiate.

I would like to briefly make a small point here. All numerical bases are equivalent in that they are bijective (they share a one-to-one correspondence). Every number can be represented in every base and in only one way in that base as a unique sequence of digits. Consequently, it doesn't make any difference which base we use for any given application. Common math uses base ten, but for maximum parsimony, I prefer base two, or binary, so for the remainder of this discussion I will consider binary numerals (also called bit strings), i.e., sequences of 0s and 1s.

Information, Matter, Energy, Entropy

As this discussion converges on topics of brain and mind, I will focus primarily on instances of information, a term given precise meaning by Claude Shannon with respect to bit strings [44]. In this form, using either Shannon's equation (all but identical to the Boltzmann thermodynamic equivalent), or using a metric like Kolmogorov complexity [23, 24], we can measure (or least conceive of) the informational content of a bit string, i.e., the shortest compressed version of the string, or alternatively, the tersest algorithm for generating the string. Both ways of conceiving of information are, at their core, essentially the same.

It is widely recognized that there is an equality between matter and energy, and even a clear mathematical transformation between the two (thank you, Einstein). What is less frequently appreciated is that there is a third concept involved: thermodynamic entropy. The truly astounding realization is that this form of entropy (which is notably a property of *physical* things like matter and energy) is closely related to Shannon and Kolmogorov notions of information with respect to bit strings [43]. As a related tangent, I recommend that the tantalized reader research *reversible computing* [26, 27].

The upshot of the implied relationship between physical entropy and information is that we can now appreciate the physical universe in informational terms. For example, just as we can look at a chunk of matter and conceptualize it as a (rather astounding) *chunk* of energy, as per Einstein, we can now appreciate that same chunk of matter for its informational content, literally some bit string[9]. Seen in this way, a crystal contains very little information whereas a handful of dirt or an arbitrary rock contains substantially more complexity. Whether this complexity translates to actual information can get a little thorny. We don't generally regard the most entropic and random of systems as containing the greatest information. Rather, the notion of information is usually preserved for a notion of a *meaningful* pattern communicated between a signaler and a receiver (who need not be people, they could be a 3D scanner and a 3D printer). All that said, if one were motivated to store the description of a crystal on one hand, and a bucket of dirt on the other, we could rightly describe the latter as containing more information than the former and as correspondingly requiring a lengthier informational description to represent its physical state.

We can quantify the information intrinsic to a given chunk of matter by considering the necessary description of that matter, the actual bit string that would represent the chunk's physical state so that, given an imaginary matter-construction-machine (an idealized nano-scale 3D printer in effect), we could create a perfect duplicate of the chunk. When I glance around my surroundings, I see physical objects not only for their material content, and not even only for their energy content, i.e., their twentieth century realized antimatter annihilation potential (god forbid), but also for their pure informational content. I see simple structures as literally embedding less information than complex structures. Viewed this way, the world's gaudiest jewel becomes the dullest and plainest manifestation of form, a veritable icon of sterility.

We need look no further than page six (still well within the prelude) of Dennett's seminal work on the consciousness to see this concept in action, albeit from a different angle [13]. Dennett opens his book with a contemplation of the infamous brain-in-a-vat scenario, in which he concludes that in order to contrive a virtual reality for the brain's mind, the mad scientists must account for a true combinatorial explosion of interactions between the mind's perception of its own fingers

---

[9] Others have apparently had similar ideas [8].

and the nigh-infinite textures, temperatures, pliabilities, etc. of the perceived, yet artificial, world. He concludes that the only feasible way to offer the brain and its mind a reasonable simulacra is to cheat and create a real physical sandbox system to initiate the relevant nerve interactions to the brain. He points out that this is precisely how flight-simulators work. They are not pure software constructions, but actual secondary cockpits, housed in gigantic boxes (rooms), in which the pilots sit during a simulation.

We can interpret Dennett's results in another way, however. Rather than consider the exponential varieties of interactions between oneself and the physical world, consider the informational embedding of that world. The reason that the brain-in-a-vat veritably requires a real physical system to emulate its larger experiences, and the reason that a realistic flight simulator requires an actual cockpit, is that these physical systems directly embed their associated abstract occurrence and their metaphysical type—which can be understood as a very long informational bit string of those physical systems' structure (down to a spatial scale required by human sensation). It is actually exceedingly difficult to cheat physical reality by way of simulation since the informational content of physical systems that must be simulated *literally is* their physical embedding. In other words, by the time the mad scientists have constructed a reasonable simulation for the brain-in-a-vat, they have all but built the physical system they intended to simulate, and so, as Dennett demonstrates à la flight simulators, they may as well just build the darn thing to begin with.

Relationship Between Tokens and Abstract Occurrences

If multiple identical tokens (multiple identical physical instances) embed common shared nonspatio-temporal types then we must conclude that materially identical objects refer to the exact same abstract and singular type. Two 5s written on a piece of paper refer to the same '5' type. They are conceptually linked through their embedding of the membership in the '5' universal type grouping or their embedding of the *5ness* universal property. Furthermore, given that for every object (i.e., token) there always exists a sibling abstract occurrence that describes the informational content of the token (some bit string), then we can say that those abstract occurrences refer to the same type as the tokens themselves. Just as two tokens, such as two 5s written on paper, reference the same type, so do an object and its associated abstract information reference the same type. It's precisely the same situation except that one of the referencing occurrences is nonspatio-temporal.

To state this differently, any token (any physical object) has an equivalent abstract occurrence, the bit string that describes its material structure, and they both refer to the same type, the same bit string— and just to complete the point, not only do an object and its abstract description reference a single shared type, but any other identical object (and its associated abstract occurrence, as a pair) also reference the same single type. All such occurrences are intimately connected through their membership in the type, an overarching bit string that anchors all the occurrences together.

Consider a perfect crystal of pure carbon (a diamond) of some specified shape and dimensions, say one centimeter along a primary edge. Now consider two such crystals sitting next to each other. For the sake of argument, they are ideal, perfect, pure, and molecularly identical down to the last atom. These two crystals both reference the exact same type (a specific diamond crystal structure, a type of matter configuration). Now consider the informational description of those cubes, which depending on the reader's choice of granularity may be as vague as the one just provided (mere dimensions and structural overview) or may be as specific as identifying every atom, or perhaps every subatomic particle, the distinguishing difference in bit string length being captured by Kolmogorov reasoning such that a terser description is allowed only because the replicating algorithm itself contains the additional information. We can easily permit a vast number of tokens, and a near infinite number abstract occurrences (say, instantiated sentences discussing and musing on these diamonds) of this exact same type. One need look no further than a box of ball bearings to get a sense for the potential multi-occurrence at play here, albeit tokenized in nature in that example.

Type/Token Ambiguity

In earlier sections, and specifically in figure 5, I showed that the mapping between a type and its tokens can be quite loose. Nevertheless, we might naively expect token separation to at least be *conceptually* complete. That is, even if many tokens can embed a given type, we might assume that it is still clear *which* type a given token actually embeds—but one of the tokens in figure 5 was a rectangular bar for heaven's sake, and another was a two-color trapezoidal flag. These examples don't inspire hope in the notion that tokens unambiguously embed their associated types. Consider figure 6, in which the same exact token (not just two identical tokens, but the same physical instance) indisputably embeds two different types! Notably, the exact same token can *mean different things* (i.e., embed different types, or carry different information) depending on context. Or consider the cavalier playfulness with which graphic artists and type-setters intentionally conflate alphanumeric characters (also a defining feature of *leetspeak*, a popular hacker motif), or the chuckle-inspiring jury-rig we have all witnessed in which a store-owner is forced to substitute for a missing 'S' on his sign when promoting a 'BIG 5ALE'.

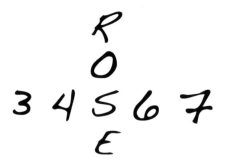

Figure 6. Type/Token ambiguity – This figure demonstrates ambiguity in type/token embedding. Not only might identical tokens embed the '5' and 'S' types, but in this case, due to the spatial arrangement, a single token actually embeds both types simultaneously (or perhaps alternately)!

There are at least two (perhaps more) solutions to the obvious challenge such ambiguity poses. The first is to recognize that such ambiguities are generally resolved by their larger context, the totality of which is nevertheless a unique token that embeds only one overarching interpretation and that of its constituent parts. For example, in figure 6, perhaps the tokens aren't the letters at all, but rather the character sequences, such that the central character's ambiguity evaporates depending on which axis you consider. The problem with this solution is that in the earlier presentation of the *rose is a rose* sentence, I already claimed that both character-level and word-level tokens are valid concepts in their own right. Letter tokens occur within words and word tokens within sentences, so we can't simply dispense with the character-level ambiguity by relying on the word-level token to resolve the problem. Put differently, the fact that there is no word-level ambiguity in figure 6 simply doesn't impact on the remaining character-level ambiguity with respect to the smaller parts. Furthermore, we could easily contrive word-level ambiguities as well, such as homographs, distinct words that are spelled the same, like *lead* (noun) and *lead* (verb), or *duck* (noun) and *duck* (verb), so tossing the responsibility for resolving the ambiguity up a level doesn't help us much. Finally, with respect to the proposal of using context to resolve ambiguity, even in an absence of larger context, a given solitary, yet confusing, token might nevertheless *mean* '5' or 'S', depending on the creator's intent, e.g., is there any ambiguity about the meaning of the figure emblazoned on Superman's suit?[10] —which brings us to the second solution.

The second solution is to project *meaning* (the assignment of a type to a given token) into the eye (or interpretation) of the beholder or creator. While this solution solves the problem, it seems distinctly wrong in the less ambiguous cases. Surely we don't require an observer's intent or interpretation to say that a piece of salt embeds the various types of *salt*, *crystal*, and *white things*, or that a black pen line drawn on paper embeds types such as *ink*, *line*, or *black things*, or that three straight lines

---

[10] Almost as if to ruin my example, the shockingly replete comic mythos actually offers numerous interpretations for Superman's logo, including an abstract family coat-of-arms, a derivation of a Native American symbol of a snake (merely coincidental to begin with the same letter as 'super'), a Kryptonian home-world symbol for *hope*, and I suspect the list goes on—but in my defense, no one has yet mistaken it for a '5'[47]! More to the point, these additional interpretations are intentional contrivances of the historical 'S' for the purpose of injecting a richer backstory for our moodier era into a character from a simpler time. The inceptive 'S' is beyond dispute.

connecting three points in a plane and not on a line embed the *triangle* type. These are structural, topological, and geometric types, and their embedding is intrinsic in their tokens. To embed *inkness*, a token need merely be made of physical ink, interpretation be damned. But some types are more abstract. The only way to embed numeral types in an intrinsic fashion is in a unary type, shown in figure 5 with Morse code dots, fingers, or pips on a die (I'm unsure about the hashes, in which both unary counting and spatial arrangement play a part). Any numerical embedding beyond unary systems requires a cultural injection of *symbols* to represent the utilized digit types. This additional information is simply not present in the token itself and immediately explains how a given token can ambiguously embed multiple types, for all the necessary information is not in the token to begin with! Some of it is *in culture* or *in the corpus of related artifacts* (all existing physical examples of the token, such as writing, architecture, art, etc.). '5's and 'S's are disambiguated by our collective decision (that decision being a kind of *information* of course) about how to embed those types in tokens, and such collective knowledge spans the totality of our culture's artifacts, and *crucially*, the tokenized knowledge embedded in our physical brains (to be discussed in the next chapter).

On one hand, token ambiguity can seem highly problematic. If we can't say that a token explicitly embeds its assigned type, then in what way does it carry the *information* of that type? What information does the central character in figure 6 convey if it doesn't unambiguously indicate its assigned type?! In a previous section I proposed that a token literally embeds the informational representation of a type, but token ambiguity frustrates such conclusions.

While it is tempting to simply say the information requires an observer, this can't possibly be correct since it would render attempts to decode previously unknown tokens a silly enterprise: why try to *decode* a token if you, as the observer, can simply choose what you want it to represent? Better yet, we could say the information is in the eye of the *creator*, and the decoder or observer's job is to deduce the intended, but missing, cultural information of the token that resided not in the token itself, but rather in the creator's mind (R. Wiley offers a book-length analysis of these issues [54]), and in so doing complete the previously incomplete informational embedding of the token at the time of observation—but such wording is venturing into remarkably nondescript territory. We can do better.

Perhaps we could discard notions of token creators and observers by simply saying that the additional information we require of a token, but which is not embedded in the token, is spread across our culture and injected from that cultural source into any given token in any given event that utilizes it. However, I don't like *that* phrasing either since it is still too far away from the grounded type-to-raw-physical-token embedding I am arduously striving for.

I propose that we describe how nonstructural types are successfully embedded via cultural agreement by saying that nonstructural information is spread across numerous tokens which act in concert to embed that type and its informational representation. The '5' numeral exists as a Platonic type regardless of the presence of minds in the universe to make any use of its *5ness*, but in order to embed '5' in a physical token there must be a distribution of that numeral information amongst many existing physical tokens (historical and existing cultural artifacts) and also quite likely—although not required[11]—amongst a collective of minds, which are tokenized as physical brains (see next chapter). Consequently, even nonstructural types like numerals are ultimately fully tokenized in physical reality via cultural artifacts and living brains, albeit in a highly distributed manner.

---

[11] What is the work of archeology if not, in essence, the attempt to reconstruct the lost information (aka, types) of dead civilizations from only their artifacts and not a single remaining living person, i.e., a brain that would embed the otherwise incomplete information and types indicated in those same artifacts?

Supervenience

Supervenience is an important concept in metaphysics, especially with respect to the relationship between types and occurrences, and most notably, tokens in particular. Here's how the Stanford Encyclopedia of Philosophy defines the concept [29]:

> *Supervenience: A set of properties A supervenes upon another set B just in case no two things can differ with respect to A-properties without also differing with respect to their B-properties. In slogan form, "there cannot be an A-difference without a B-difference".*

Supervenience can be a little difficult to wrap one's head around. Here's a really simple restatement of the basic idea. If mind supervenes on brain, then two minds that differ by a little bit (say, your mind separated in time by five minutes) must be associated with two brains that *actually differ too* (say, the physical state of your brain separated by five minutes). So, if one wishes to claim that mind supervenes upon brain, then they are claiming that for two minds to differ, the brains that ostensibly gave rise to those minds must differ as well.

Supervenience is not symmetric. So, just because one might claim that mind supervenes on brain does not require that brain supervene on mind. In other words, we could claim that differences between minds must derive from differences in brains, and yet still permit that differences in brains not necessarily yield different minds. Supervenience certainly *could* be symmetric in this manner, but it would consist of two unrelated and coincidental instances of supervenience. For example, locations supervene on photographs since a difference in location requires that photographs of those locations must also differ, but the opposite is not true. Photographs do not supervene on locations since two different photographs don't necessarily require a difference in their associated locations; they could be two photographs of the same location, say a mountain, from different vantage points.

On one hand, it would seem to be pretty straightforward how supervenience applies to types and tokens. Types could conceivably supervene on their associated tokens, meaning that two different types would, by definition, require distinct tokens. However, as we just saw in the last section, and especially in figure 6, this is not necessarily the case. Two different types, say '5' and 'S', can, in fact, be embedded in the same token with an ambiguity (an incompleteness of embedded information) that is only resolved by either a localized context of surrounding tokens (shown to be a problematic solution) or, better yet, the collective tokenized information of the associated culture. So types don't supervene on tokens. Likewise, tokens don't supervene on types either, since figure 5 demonstrates tokens whose rather remarkable differences do not ultimately imply a difference in their embedded types (they all embed the '5' numeral). Consequently, supervenience, though a crucial topic in philosophy, and specifically in philosophy of mind, appears to have practically nothing to say about general type/token relationships. However, as we saw above, with respect to location types and photograph tokens, it clearly applies to certain *specific* type/token cases. It may, therefore, have something to say about our primary topic of interest as well, minds and brains.

There are two problems with which to contend, namely the two directions implied by the symmetry question: should type differences require token differences, and contrarily, should token differences require type differences? We can analyze these two issues separately.

The less serious issue, because it is generally less problematic in philosophy of mind, is supervenience of the physical upon the metaphysical, i.e., the requirement that differences between tokens indicate differences between their embedded types. As shown in the previous paragraph, such supervenience does not apply to general types and tokens, and is partially explained by appreciating that there may be a fairly course required spatial fidelity of a token in order to embed a given type (consider the variations in Arabic script shown in figure 5, which all embed the same Arabic symbol type for the '5' digit, despite impressive spatial variability in style). What about the more specific question of brains and minds? Within philosophy of mind, the proposal that supervenience not apply from brains to minds is often referred to as *multiple realizability*, the claim that varying physical states (brains) may embed the same metaphysical entity (mind) [4]. Multiple realizability has been presented as a crucial argument in favor of strong artificial intelligence, since strong AI would require that computers, being materially quite different from biological brains, be capable of producing and experiencing genuine mindful and conscious states. This is a straightforward rewording of the claim that brains do not supervene upon minds, since it claims that differing brains (biological vs. computerized) might embed the same mind[12].

Quantifying multiple realizability in terms of a maximum required spatial fidelity (essentially detail or feature resolution) doesn't merely apply to nonstructural types like numerals or fairly simple types like digits. It can also apply to actual structural objects. For example, the structural types associated with a crystal of pure carbon range from the purely geometric (a summary description of edge-lengths and related parameters) to the atomic (positions of every carbon atom) right through to the subatomic (states of various electrons, perhaps even quarks, although one would hope that such ridiculousness finally terminates in the vicinity of the Planck length). The notion that we can regard all tokens that are conceptually identical above a specified spatial scale as embedding the same type will be important in the next chapter, for it will enable us to regard brain-states (frozen brains) that are only identical above a certain scale (i.e., quality of brain scan) as embedding the same mind-state. Without this concept, we would have to require brain copies, scans, uploads, etc. to be perfect down to truly ludicrous scales in order to consider them as embedding the same mind-state—and that presumption would severely hamper attempts at successful uploading.

Needless to say, when we refer to disparate tokens that are considered identical above some scale for the embedding of a particular type, we are admitting that the cutoff in spatial resolution is specific to

---

[12] One might theorize that multiple realizability not necessarily have to permit a biological and computerized brain to embed the *exact same mind* (tantamount to *non*-supervenience of brains upon minds, a clear requirement of mind-uploading) but rather merely permit biological and computerized brains to embed similar *kinds* of minds (which might be compatible with full-blown supervenience while still precluding mind-uploading), a notion I won't consider in greater detail here since I have no idea how to quantify the similarity, or lack thereof, of possible *kinds of minds*.

the type. The necessary resolution for Arabic script is some feature-scale, probably in terms of the relative positions of the lines and curves composing a given character. As another example, a cat token (a living cat meowing right in front of you) embeds the cat type at a level of physiological detail requisite to distinguish it from the dog type, but also embeds the quadruped type as a much higher level of anatomical and property abstraction. Details of feline anatomy are not required in the identification and labeling of a quadruped, and in point of fact, that level of abstraction would of course include the dog where the lower level cat requirements would exclude it. In other words, some types require their associated tokens to be specified at a deeper level of detail. I don't see this observation as challenging to my thesis in any way.

The more serious issue with regard to supervenience is the question of whether a difference in type requires a difference in token. This is more serious specifically because physical and material philosophies of mind often consider as a fundamental requirement that differences in mind-states should derive exclusively from differences in underlying physical brain-states. The reasoning is fairly clear. If such supervenience were not the case—if minds could differ without an associated difference in their brains—then from where would the apparent differences in mind-states derive without resorting to substance or Cartesian dualism[13], which in modern times is not a serious option.

As we have seen, à la figure 6, type-to-token supervenience clearly doesn't apply in some cases, i.e., different types can be embedded in absolutely identical tokens (or even in the same exact token, as shown in the figure). Two solutions to this problem have been presented: one, to extend the type's tokenization to its surrounding context of nearby tokens, and two, to extend the token to the pan-cultural artifacts (the entirety of related tokens assigned to embed the given type, e.g., all writing samples of a particular letter, number or symbol), and even extend it to the tokenized brains of the members of that culture so as to include the additional information that resides in the brains and minds of the people who use those tokens.

---

[13] The theory that minds are the product of two completely different sources, a physical brain and a supernatural elixir, which conspire together to produce a mind.

Both of these solutions are problematic in the case of resolving multi-mind-to-single-brain associations since: one, there is no further context of nearby tokens to consider in conjunction with a brain (unlike the ambiguous character in figure 6, which can be extended to its enclosing character sequences), and two, there is no cultural ethos of symbol-meaning-assignment relevant to the disambiguation of otherwise identical brains; no third party is even relevant to the interpretation of a given brain (*although we might theorize that one's stance on this claim is **positively central** to the uploading question!*).

A detailed analysis should wait until after the next chapter, which extends type/token metaphysics to minds and brains, but in short, I suspect the best solution to the conundrum that written-character token ambiguity might imply mind/brain token ambiguity is simply to regard supervenience as apropos to some type/token pairs (minds and brains) but not necessarily to other pairs (as is apparently true of written characters). In defense of this conclusion, there may be no good reason to assume that ambiguity in some cases proves an ambiguity in other cases.

Minds

From Metaphysics to Minds

The astute reader will have extrapolated my reasoning far ahead by this point, but I will trudge on at the plodding speed of the written word nonetheless. Discarding theories of mind which rely on supernatural or other causes entering from beyond the brain (which would include certain branches of dualism of course), we are left with theories in which the mind arises solely from the brain. The brain is a purely physical thing of course, a confluence of atoms, molecules—cells. It is, most basically, a chunk of matter, not remarkably unlike any other physical object in this respect. Consequently, it can be represented informationally as a description of its physical state at any given moment, or as a sequence of such states over time, namely a description in the form of a bit string. In fact, modern medicine endeavors toward such goals with great enthusiasm as the diversity and fidelity of various brain-scanning technology steadily evolve.

The underlying premise of such scanning technologies is that the salient aspects of the brain (i.e., the aspects we are interested in for a given application, such as associating brain physiology with mental phenomena) are surely there to be captured in such scans in the first place—but what is a *scan* if not a procedure to capture the informational representation of a physical object, i.e., to infer from a token its associated abstract occurrence? This leads to a profound conclusion: we saw above that if multiple occurrences coexist (including the possibility of multiple tokens), then they all refer to a single shared type—and we must extend that conclusion to brains and whatever type it is that they instantiate, i.e., two identical brains refer to a single *type* of some sort.

We can conceptualize the type that the brain refers to in a few ways. On one level, the informational version of a brain is simply the structural blue-print for creating the brain, and has no *mindful* properties at all, but rather is a description of which atoms go where to make a perfect material copy (a second token) of that brain. On the other hand, a brain itself offers multiple levels of interpretation. It is not just an object, but one which exhibits a particular set of properties, and it is those properties that we define as a *mind*—and those properties are likewise captured in the informational form, the abstract occurrence—the brain scan. So we can say the scan encodes the mind as well as the brain, for the scan has captured the required components to reproduce both brain and mind properties in a second physical instance (a second brain), barring an incompatible Cartesian or substance dualistic theory of mind, which we aren't considering here.

Admittedly, my conceptualization of types, tokens, and the information that ties them together is a veritable restatement of *pattern identity theory* [31], namely that a person's identity (or anything's identity for that matter) is synonymous with the pattern of their structural material embedding and not with the material components themselves (thus, a chess position is identified by its piece-placement, and not by the wood or stone (see figure 7)). Pattern identity claims that two brains which embed the same pattern identify the same mind-state—bearing in mind that brains and minds are typically not frozen, but rather dynamic, a nuance which is discussed at length in this book. Observe that pattern identity as presented here closely aligns with the token/type embedding presented in figure 5. Like figure 5, a given pattern (aka, type) can reside at a fairly high level of abstraction relative to the fidelity of its embedding: figure 5 showed a wide variety of '5' tokens while figure 7 shows the same chess pattern (a metaphysical *type*) embedded in considerably different depictions of chess boards—but not *arbitrarily* different; namely, they remain similar enough to both embed the pattern in question.

Figure 7. Pattern identity of chess positions – According to pattern identity theory, these two depictions of the end of Game 1 between Kasparov and Deep Blue both embed the same game *identity*, i.e., the same actual game, even though they are so radically different as to actually reside in different numbers of spatial dimensions. Note that this conclusion of same identity is in accordance with how we commonly refer to famous chess games, namely in their singular form, as employed in this very caption in fact.

It is remarkable how hostile people can be to pattern identity. The first attack is generally a quick accusation of unspecified dualism, since dualism is regarded with fairly universal contempt (see later discussion). Of course, practically without exception, adherents of identity theory patently reject materially incompatible flavors of dualism (and I prefer to avoid dualistic labels entirely, for specifically the reason of this kind of confusion).

Note that these conclusions can only be true of frozen (or static) brains (with the exception of The White Room experiment, described below). Recall from the glossary that a frozen brain need not necessarily be literally frozen (which is why I also use the term static for the same concept). Rather, the notion of a frozen brain implies a brain undergoing no dynamic processes, a brain that is in stasis (I occasionally refer to a static spatio-temporal object as merely spatial but not truly temporal, or as residing *outside* time). Therefore, we needn't concern ourselves with whether two *conscious* brains (two awake people, two uploads, an original and one upload, whatever) embed the same mind. By being conscious, they definitively preclude an identical physical embedding since they are in a constant state of dynamic flux, and therefore cannot conceivably refer to the same abstract mind (caveat The White Room, to be presented shortly). But if they are frozen then we can seriously consider the proposal that they do, in fact, reference a single shared mind—for as long as they remain static. This necessity to carefully disambiguate static and dynamic processes may explain much of the rancor over identity theory; the various parties may simply be talking past one another on these subtler distinctions.

So, if two brains are in static states, i.e., brain-states, be they biological, upload, or one of each, and given that they implicitly encode their own abstract occurrences, i.e., the informational description of those brains, and given that all four occurrences, two physical and two abstract, refer to the same non-multiexisting mind type (literally a bit string describing the state of the mind), then we conclude that they actually refer to the same mind—so long as they remain static and therefore identical in state.

The White Room

To extend the conclusion just described, we can consider a rather extreme thought experiment, which I call *The White Room*. Let us assume that physical determinism is, in fact, true[14]. Let us imagine two sufficiently identical physical environments, such as diffusely-lit white rooms populated with minimalistic furniture and geometric objects, to offer a reasonable variety of interactions but not be so complicated that our expectations of determinism should easily break down. If our two static brains (with bodies, i.e., people or uploads) are placed in these two identical environments, and within a deterministic universe, then we can permit them to become dynamic again (to wake up). That is to

---

[14] Even from the perspective of quantum mechanics, determinism is currently wildly contentious, as evidenced by any casual survey of the ongoing debate [21], but our thought experiment is purely hypothetical and we will assume a deterministic universe.

say, from this starting position, we can then permit them to resume consciousness and continue *running*—or to become *embedded within time* as I like to say.

In this scenario, the brains will receive identical sensory input, will perform identical internal processing, and will produce identical external (and internal) behavior as they walk around the room and interact with the various objects. They will operate in lock-step indefinitely, not only for seconds or minutes, but for years or decades. They will behave identically not only in their external behavior but in their moment-to-moment internal self-reflection. They aren't even necessarily isolated from the rest of the universe; we can, for example, interact with them through a system that guarantees identical simultaneous interactions, such as an electronic audio-visual system (video-chatting). Whatever we speak into our microphone will be heard by both subjects at the same time. Whatever image we present to the camera will be seen at the same time, and the experiment suggests that they will speak back and appear back on their respective cameras to our two screens in perfect unison, not only for a minute or two, but for the rest of their lives. Even if we look to our left to view the screen showing one subject and to our right to the view the other, there is no way for us to ever communicate to the subjects who is who or to otherwise assist them in disentangling their existences.

By my interpretation, the reasoning presented earlier suggests that these two conscious and awake minds, perhaps two biological clones, two ordinary people for all intents and purposes, actually embed the same mind (the same metaphysical mind type), albeit in two distinct metaphysical tokens (bodies and brains)! This is an astounding conclusion and I suspect that despite the rigor with which I have presented it, most readers will nevertheless reject it, insisting that two conscious people must, regardless of any theory or circumstances, embed distinct minds—even if they are absolutely physically identical. So be it; I have tried my best. Given that determinism may very well be false anyway, we needn't concern ourselves with this scenario further, but it is worth remembering as we proceed. I will leave it here and move on, for there are yet other matters to consider.

Splitting a Mind

In the next few sections, I present perhaps only one of a small number of significantly novel aspects of my philosophy. (Others include my views on free-will, to be presented toward the end of this book, and perhaps a third contribution if I can claim credit for The White Room, although I wouldn't be surprised if someone else has conceived of such a scenario before.) Much of what I have written so far is not particularly revolutionary as it has consisted primarily of views that have probably been considered previously. Quite the contrary, what I have presented up to this point is a summary of Platonic realism, a very cursory overview of information theory, and some implications for brains and minds. Previous sections merely set the stage for a presentation of my primary theory on this topic: that minds are capable of *splitting* evenly into multiple distinct minds.

One of the most profound implications of the reasoning laid out so far is that one mind can give the appearance of arbitrarily splitting into two or more distinct minds, multiple descendants of a single common ancestral mind. I will employee the terminology of *splitting* to a significant degree, speaking of a single mind splitting into multiple descendants. Curiously, as we explore this idea in detail, we will see that the notion of *splitting* is actually a misnomer, although I maintain its use due to its conceptual simplicity.

Brains, Brain-States, Minds, Mind-States

Consider a biological brain. It represents a token (a physical occurrence, i.e., actual matter), tightly coupled with a corresponding abstract occurrence that represents the information content of the brain's physical structure. Both of these occurrences, one physical and one nonspatio-temporal, embed an abstract type. What should we call this type? The immediate suggestion might be to call it a mind, that is to say that a brain is a token of the mind type, but we have overlooked the crucial temporal aspect of both these entities and in so doing have convoluted the issue. A brain is not merely spatial, but spatio-temporal. Sure, we can freeze a brain, thus rendering it static, but in so doing we eliminate the fundamental aspects of what it means to be a brain. To be a brain is hardly to be the requisite chunk of matter in a static state. To a significantly greater degree, to be a brain is to undergo the dynamic process of brain function and behavior. Even when we do consider a static brain to *be a brain*, it is only in so far as the static version holds the promise of its dynamic behavioral potential. This observation is true of anything that fundamentally involves dynamic processes. For example, consider a bird momentarily interrupted in mid-flight, suspended in the air seemingly immune to gravity. In what sense would such a bird be *in flight*? Consider a popped balloon partway through its resulting explosion, shards of rubber suspended in air but not actually moving. Does such a system truly tokenize the concept of explosion, or must the dynamic aspect of the explosion be permitted to proceed through time in order for the explosion to be fully realized? Metabolism, walking, growing, flowing water, tornados, the list goes on and the interpretation is the same: dynamic processes cannot be meaningfully considered in transitory static states. Likewise, brains involve dynamic processes as a fundamental property of their definition and we must therefore take those dynamic processes into account when appreciating what brain tokenization truly represents.

A brain can be described as a sequence of tokenized brain-states, each brain-state simply encoding a static physical configuration of brain structure. Note that this definition of brain differs from the colloquial definition, which would be better described as one of two things:

1. Either a nontemporal-but-spatial tokenized brain-state (a definition which accounts for the fact that we would generally describe a literal frozen brain sitting in a freezer *as being a brain*).
2. Or as the dynamic structure that embeds and exhibits brain-states (how we would describe the living biological organ, what we generally mean when we casually refer to *the brain*).

The concept of a brain is difficult to describe in metaphysical terms because occurrences (and tokens are a kind of occurrence) are generally static since they embed a type and types are themselves generally conceptually static. Consequently, neither types nor tokens easily accommodate dynamic traits, such as we colloquially presume of living brains. Therefore, I will forgo colloquial usage and use the definition I have offered instead: *a brain is a type consisting of a sequence (ostensibly a temporal sequence) of brain-state types* and a brain token is a sequence of tokenized brain-states.

The brain-states themselves are not really the brain, nor do they individually map to a full mind, but rather are mere *parts* of a brain, parts in time as opposed to parts in space, as it were. A brain itself does not exist *at a given time* but rather spans time itself. Likewise, a mind is temporal (although not spatial). A mind is a sequence of mind-states and a brain is a sequence of brain-states. The correspondences align quite nicely, mind-states to brain-states, and mind to brain. Note that this isn't the first time mind or consciousness have been described as a series of discrete states, like frames in a movie [46]. To bring this all with the fold of metaphysical terminology, *a mind is a type consisting of a sequence of mind-state types*[15], very much like a numeral is a type consisting of a sequence of digit types. In the case of mind, the sequence is temporal, while in the case of numerals, the sequence is distributed along a spatial dimension (e.g., left to right), but the distinction is specious since entities that naturally reside in time can be transformed to reside in space by utilizing an additional spatial dimension to encode and represent the time dimension. We do this all the time when we convert audio (say, music) to a recording by converting the temporal

---

[15] One might ask what temporal resolution is expected of minds: how many mind-states occur per second or of what duration is a mind-state? Although such considerations are irrelevant to the abstract philosophical considerations presented here, there is tenuous evidence that mind-states may occur at a spacing of ~10–20ms (~100Hz) [17], or perhaps upwards of 100ms [46]. These rates are tantalizingly close to action potential emission rates (see §1.1.1.2). In other words, perhaps we need each action potential (from a given neuron, not the entire brain of course) to be encoded within a new mind-state, or put differently, we need any given mind-state to not be required to encode two action potentials from the same neuron. This description feels loosely like Fourier analysis of a smooth signal via discrete sampling at or above the Nyquist rate. All of these conclusions are wildly speculative however—and as stated, totally irrelevant to our larger discussion.

dimension of audio to an additional spatial dimension, such as the length of an audio tape, the groove of a vinyl record, the track of a compact disc or computer drive, etc.

While a mind type is a sequence of mind-states, an instantiated sequence is a mind, namely an occurrence of a sequence of mind-state occurrences within a nonspatial but temporal domain. Brains are similar, but the terminology is more token-heavy. In conventional metaphysics, the temporal aspect of tokens is often ignored. An apple is casually said to be a token of the apple type, disregarding any dynamic processes. Curiously, to even speak of the apple is to consider its intrinsic spatio-temporal existence, its tokenization at a spatio-temporal *coordinate* (the apple exists exactly right there right now, it doesn't just generally exist), but since an apple is relatively static, and since its various subtly dynamic behavior (growing or rotting) is practically never considered in metaphysical pondering, the implications of the temporal embedding are generally hand-waved and philosophers blithely call an apple a token of an apple type and move on to other topics—but in the case of brains we simply must consider the temporal dimension more carefully. It is not sufficient to merely say that a brain is a token of the brain type, because such a statement ignores (or at least utterly glosses over) the brain's essential dynamic properties (i.e., that it constantly changes state over time). One might see a parallel here with Heraclitus' dictum that *"you cannot step into the same river twice."*

Therefore, by definition, the brain is in constant flux and its variation from moment to moment must maintain eminence in the discussion. So be it. We can now map between brains and minds, as shown in tables 2 and 3 and figure 8.

Note that a brain-state token is tantamount to a frozen brain. If we literally freeze a biological brain, we can then glimpse the brain-state token embedded in physical reality that resides at the front of the brain's temporal queue. That brain-state maps directly to a corresponding mind-state abstract occurrence, an occurrence of the mind-state type. When we consider frozen brains, we have the opportunity to consider the properties of brains and minds with disregard for the temporal dimension, and this can greatly ease our analysis.

Brain metaphysical concept	Mind metaphysical concept
Brain-state type a **type** of physical structure	**Mind-state type** a **type** of mental phenomena
Brain type a **type** of sequence of brain-states	**Mind type** a **type** of sequence of mind-states
Brain-state token a spatial occurrence of brain-state type	**Mind-state abstract occurrence** an abstract occurrence of mind-state type
Brain token a spatio-temporal occurrence of brain type	**Mind abstract occurrence** a temporal occurrence of mind type

Table 2. Mapping between metaphysical brain and mind – This table presents the mapping between the various brain and mind metaphysical concepts. The two domains connected by the mapping are brute physical brains and their corresponding nonphysical minds. Each domain houses four layers: two *types*, one for an instant in time and one for a sequence of such instances, and two *occurrences*, one of each type.

Brain concept	S/T Aspect	Mind concept	S/T Aspect
Brain-state type	DS, NT	Mind-state type	NS, NT
Brain type	DS, DT	Mind type	NS, DT
Brain-state token	S, NT	Mind-state abstract occurrence	NS, NT
Brain token	S, T	Mind abstract occurrence	NS, T

Table 3. Spatio-temporal aspects of brain and mind – This table shows the spatial and temporal aspects of the various brain and mind metaphysical concepts. Please refer to the included legend.

	Yes	No	No but descriptive
Spatial	S	NS	DS
Temporal	T	NT	DT

For example, the brain-state type is nonspatial but describes a spatially instantiable concept (a brain-state, i.e., a frozen brain), so it is labeled DS.

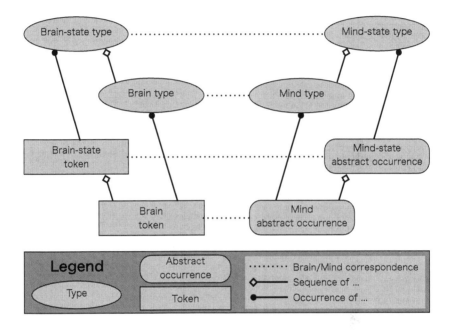

Figure 8. Relationships of brain & mind metaphysical entities –
This figure shows the various metaphysical entities of brain and
mind and how they relate to one another. For example, the brain
type consists of a sequence of brain-state types and may occur (be
instantiated as) a spatio-temporal brain token.

Realism of Numerals

I said above that we can conceive of minds as *splitting*, then claimed that this notion is a misnomer, then claimed that I would use the term *split* anyway since I find the basic idea to be helpful in conceptualizing various mind-uploading scenarios. These points will be clarified in the next section, but first, let us consider the issue of *when* or *under what circumstances* we may consider a type to actually exist. This deep question cuts to the core of metaphysical philosophy, dividing two of the greatest players of the game, Plato and Aristotle. With respect to universals (not specifically types) they disagreed on this point. Plato's position, called Platonic realism, states that universals exist in their own right (admittedly nonspatio-temporally) regardless of the existence of tokens that would reference those universals. Essentially, Plato claimed that types exist eternally, never arising and never vanishing. Aristotle's alternative, Aristotelian realism, states that universals exist but only in so far as they are invoked by particulars (essentially tokens). In other words, if nothing in the entire universe were sharp, then sharpness as a concept would not (or could not) exist. Likewise, while sharpness may exist so long as sharp things exist, if the last sharp thing vanishes, then sharpness vanishes with it.

Translating the Platonic/Aristotelian disagreement from universals and particulars to types and tokens, we get the following questions: Do types really exist, and eternally so, apart from any association with physical spatio-temporal reality (Platonic realism) or do they only exist when manifested by an occurrence (Aristotelian realism), either abstract or token? Furthermore, is an abstract occurrence sufficient to invoke a type or is a token required? One could also ask whether abstract occurrences exist in a Platonic way or whether they are subject to the same limitations as Aristotelian types, only existing when mapped onto some underlying token?

With the questions now posed, I will constrain it to a particular set of types and occurrences: numerals, namely binary numerals, since these are sufficient to represent all more complex types anyway (and with greatest parsimony). That is to say that in the same way that binary numerals are isomorphic to all higher-base numerals, likewise any numeral of any base is also isomorphic to any other type that we would not generally conceive of as numerals, such as text, pictures, audio, video, or physical three dimensional structure like sculpture or statuary—or brains of course. All of these things can be represented as bit strings. If the reader holds any doubt about this claim, simply recall that such a mapping is precisely how modern computers work. They are capable of encoding any *type* of information, and the reason they can do that is that all information can be reduced to bit strings.

We can now confine all our subsequent analysis to one very specific type: binary sequences. Here then, is the question posed in the new context: Does every single conceivable binary sequence already exist, as a unique type in and of itself (Platonism), or alternatively, does any given binary sequence, say 100010101101, not really exist as a type until it is first embedded either in an abstract occurrence or a physical token (Aristotelianism), as I just did with one particular sequence in this very sentence?

The Library of Anaxagoras

I have said that I describe mind-uploading as a split, but that I admit it is not necessarily a perfectly accurate term. Let's see what's actually going on. Consider the space of all possible mind-state types, i.e., mind-state space. We can, of course, conceive of an equivalent concept, brain-state space. This idea has been applied in the past to other topics. For example, there is Jorge Luis Borges' Library of Babel [5], which contains all possible books under a designated maximum length and, there is Daniel Dennett's Library of Mendel [14], which contains all possible genetic sequences and by extension all possible species. Brain-state space is simply the space of all possible structural configurations of a biological brain at some specified physical or component scale, say atomic, molecular or perhaps a higher-level description of neurological state. Mind-state space (or the *Library of Anaxagoras*, if I may coin the term[16]) holds every conceivable mind-state type (or equivalent bit

---

[16] Anaxagoras is the pre-Socratic Greek philosopher who first gave us the idea of *nous*, or mind [9], although his exact usage only loosely fits that used here.

string), i.e., every conceivable conglomeration of mental phenomena that could denote a unique mind-state, namely a mind at any time in its life (see figure 9). By mental phenomena I intend the totality of experiences, memory, and other acquired knowledge or skill, logical or emotional in nature, from hallowed intellectual to rote motor, conscious or unnoticed, that represents a mind at a given moment in its life—but for simplicity's sake, simply consider the set of memories (all the other aspects of mental state can be interpreted as various forms of *memory*, i.e., neural encoding). As far as I can tell this conceptualization of memory is essentially identical to that used by Hayworth [20].

To pursue this idea further, each point in mind-state space describes the memories and consequent cognitive state of a mind at some point in its life, and the total space contains every point in every life of every person who could ever live, namely in all the times and places that any person ever could live. Not only does it include the moment-to-moment states of everyone who ever actually lived (and everyone who will actually live in the future), but it also includes fantastical yet sensorially sensible experiences such as your being suddenly and inexplicably transported to ancient Egypt to live the remainder of your days, and it includes some actual historical Egyptian (now lost to the sands of obscurity) being suddenly transported to a modern city, not due to the possibility of time travel, but simply because the underlying chronological series of sensory experiences (a lifetime of visual scenery) is entirely physically plausible in a teleportation-like fashion. It includes you (and me, and everyone else) hypothetically living on a planet on the far side of the universe, or in a space station, or on the surface of a neutron star—and by far the most spectacular realization, mind-state space also includes every point in the imaginary lives of the truly countless people who have never ever existed at all.

The Library of Anaxagoras is big.

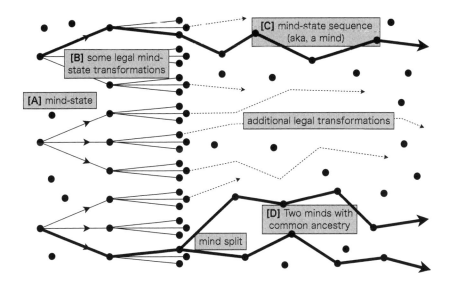

Figure 9. Mind-state space (The Library of Anaxagoras) – This figure depicts mind-state space, which contains all possible mind-states (shown as dots [A]). From any given mind-state it is possible to transform through sufficiently small (i.e., legal) transformations to numerous other mind-states (shown as edges [B]). Observe that transformations are *directed*, meaning they can only be traversed in one direction, namely forward in time, or cumulative in experience and memory. Additionally, any given mind-state can only be reached *from* at most one other mind-state (see text for explanation). Temporal sequences of mind-states represent plausible individual minds (shown with thick edges [C]). Two such sequences sharing a common ancestry, but splitting at some point, typify nondestructive mind-uploading (shown along the bottom of the figure [D]). Curiously, even though mind-states, being metaphysical types, are definitively nontemporal entities (to say nothing of being overtly nonspatial), and even though minds are also nontemporal as types, they nevertheless describe temporally embedded concepts (see table 3), a feature which is readily observed in the figure as a directionality through mind-state space from left to right. This property can even impose a certain *relative* temporal ordering on mind-states. That is to say, while mind-states do not have absolute temporal *coordinates*, pairs of mind-states within a given mind sequence share a relative temporal relation to one another.

Transformations

Switching back to brain-states momentarily, we can consider not only the individual coordinates in brain-state space (those coordinates being brain-state types and describing momentary physical brain structure), but also which other brain-state types we can reach from a given brain-state via some epsilon transformation, i.e., which states differ by a *tiny* amount (this idea also indicates the dimensionality of the space). With regard to character sequences (strings), such transformations are called *Hamming distance 1* and consist of altering a single position in the string (flipping a single bit in the case of bit strings) [18]. In the Library of Babel, such transformations consist of a single character replacement in an entire book (which is, of course, a character string), and in the Library of Mendel, such transformations consist of a single base mutation in an entire genetic sequence (which are, of course, also strings of a sort). The point is to consider pairs of brain-state types that are directly adjacent in brain-state space. What would this epsilon difference in brain-state space actually be? The answer is whatever precision of physical structure encoding we have assumed for brain-states. If that precision is, say, atomic, then a single transformation would be a subtle change in a single atom in the brain, say its energy level, or its bond (or lack-thereof) to a nearby neighbor. Alternatively, if we say the precision is neural, then a single transformation could be the presence or absence of a single action potential or something to that effect. Crucially, it is nowhere near possible to directly connect any arbitrary pair of brain-states; virtually all brain-state pairs are far too different to transfer directly between. Only those pairs of brain-states differing by this minuscule epsilon are considered adjacent.

Note that certain transformations are subject to the *arrow of time*, which means they aren't reversible [15]. If a transformation from state A to B consists of the conduction of a single action potential, then we can't transform from B back to A within the physical limits imposed by neurology.

Since our epsilon transformation could be affected upon any atom or neuron in the brain, we can easily conceive that a given brain-state can transform through brain-state space to a truly vast number of next brain-states. Question: Is it equally true that a given brain-state could have evolved *from* a vast number of brain-states elsewhere in brain-state space? Well, conceivably, any atom or neuron might be the one whose epsilon change brought about the current brain-state from the previous state, so the answer would appear to be *vast* as I have put it; a brain-state could both evolve forward with great diversity and could also have followed a great diversity of prior brain-states.

Now let's consider mind-states, which are isomorphic with brain-states (one-to-one correspondence). True enough, a given mind-state could evolve to a tremendous number of next mind-states (see figure 9, although for comprehension it only depicts a dearth of the true variability in this regard). To comprehend the scale of possible transformations from one mind-state to the next, realize that mind-states are dictated not only by various internal processing but also by external sensory stimuli. Thus, we can imagine exposing the senses (let's consider vision) to any arbitrary input pattern from one mind-state to the next. Ordinarily this would not occur; our visual experience would represent a smooth flow of steady visual changes—but this is not a physical restriction. A simple example of the contrary case involves a television or computer screen, which could easily display practically any imaginable visual scene to our eyes from one moment to the next. This diversity translates directly into the variety of ways in which one mind-state could evolve to the next state; it is all but infinite. Consider the space of all possible visual sensations a person can experience, literally every visual scene (picture) a person could ever witness, whether photorealistic, cartoonish, artistically abstract, or utterly pixelated noise[17]. Curiously, the breadth of the space of all possible visual scenes is, in fact, smaller than the number of mind-states one state could transition to since all of those visual scenes must then be multiplied by the diversity of other sensory phenomena as well (hearing, smell, etc.). And yet, a mind-state can only transition to a tiny fraction of the total available

[17] To grasp the scope of all such images, consider that a 16:9 HDTV (1920×1080 px) screen, even if using only 8-bit color (e.g., 4:2:2 YCbCr), can display $256^{2073600}$ unique images, most of which are just noise of course, but which could nevertheless influence a mind-state transition in subtle ways. For comparison, note that there are a scant 10^{80} atoms in the universe.

mind-states, namely only those differing by our prescribed epsilon. Most mind-states are too different for direct transition.

One might ask what constitutes an epsilon change with regard to mind-states. What metric could signify a minuscule difference between momentary mental phenomena? This is admittedly a much more convoluted issue than in the case of tangible brain-states. Thankfully, we can dispense with this matter by remembering that mind-states are isomorphic with brain-states. Therefore, whatever mental or psychological concept ultimately quantifies a mind-state epsilon will simply derive from the underlying brain-states and *their* epsilon differences. This realization doesn't necessarily help us conceptualize or visualize epsilon differences in mind-states, but alleviates any potential *concern* over the matter by passing it to its simpler cousin, brain-state epsilons.

So a mind-state can evolve forward in time with astounding diversity, just like a brain-state. However, how many mind-states could a given mind-state have evolved *from*? When posed for brain-states, this question yielded a similarly vast diversity. Astoundingly, in the case of mind-states, and with a caveat to be described below, the answer is precisely one! A mind-state can only have evolved from exactly one other mind-state in the near-infinite space of all possible mind-states! This truly gobsmacking conclusion is actually rather simple to understand. Recall that a mind-state can be conceptualized as a recording of all surviving memories (see the section *The Library of Anaxagoras* for a clarification of what I mean by *memory*) from birth (or slightly earlier) to the present—and there can only be one such sequence of memories converging on a given mind-state, i.e., a given mind at a given point in its life. The exact same mind-state cannot encode two different sets of memories. To do so would be to remember your life in two different ways, both of which are remembered as equally valid. How many ways could your life have brought you to this very moment, your precise mental and memory configuration? How many ways could you remember you life as it has actually transpired? How many ways could you have lived your life and still have it be precisely the same life you have actually lead? The answer is clearly one. Figure 10 summarizes these concepts.

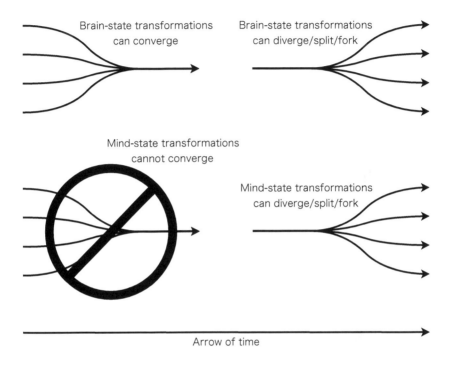

Figure 10. Brain-state and mind-state transformations – This figure shows the kinds of transformations that are possible through brain-state space and mind-state space. Notably, multiple mind-states cannot realistically transition to the same mind-state forward in time, but divergence in entirely conceivable, and in fact is required by both nondeterminism and/or free-will.

Now, to be sure, memory is extremely imprecise, foggy, incomplete, and rife with contradictions, forgetfulness, and self-doubt, which would seem to suggest that we might have followed multiple paths to get to our current state—but *all* of those feelings and deviations from perfect memory are encoded in the current mind-state. The doubt or forgetfulness you feel about a particular period of time in your past (I'm referring to the sense of doubt itself, not the faded memory) is itself recorded in your current mind-state. That doubt is a part of you since you can sense it, but that doubt is a causal result of the faded memory—so a given mind-state could only have followed precisely one earlier mind-state. In short, the notion that a mind-state essentially encodes its entire history definitively precludes two different sequences from ever converging on the same mind-state.

Admittedly, there is a conceptual caveat to the notion that a mind-state can only arise from one possible prior mind-state. It is just barely conceivable that as memories fade to absolute and total obscurity, two paths through mind-state space could converge on an identical state. However, such a convergence requires the subset of their respective memories that differ and are forgotten to truly and utterly disappear, not just higher-order cognitively, but neurologically down to the last neuron, the last synapse, perhaps even the last molecule. We are talking about the most complete amnesia imaginable. Not a single cognitive causal effect can survive (what in the corresponding brain-state would amount to any structural change at all); the two underlying brain-states must be structurally identical despite having had different experiences over the courses of their lives. While this notion may be a logical possibility within the rules of mind-state and associated brain-state transitions, and therefore be worthy of brief mention, it is a practical impossibility in natural experience. Therefore, to a first approximation, we can proceed on the assumption that mind-states can arise from only one other state in the total space.

To paraphrase the conclusions from above, minds can split forward in time (see the sequence along the bottom edge of figure 9, or see figure 10), but may never split backward in time. Another way to phrase it is that minds can split forward in time but can never merge forward in time, while they can merge backward in time but can never split backward in time.

If by chance we have two occurrences of the same mind, i.e., two occurrences of the same mind-type at a given moment in time (and two associated tokens of the underlying brain-states, i.e., actual brains of some sort), then when those two minds consciously (i.e., wakefully) and dynamically evolve to the next mind-state in their respective sequences, they will certainly appear to *split* into two different sequences with identical sequence histories up to the last moment in time, and then suddenly diverge into two unique mind-states.

This belabored method of conceptualizing the issue is where my coinage of the term *splitting minds* comes from. At the same time it illustrates why the notion of splitting is something of a misnomer, since any given mind does not really split into two minds (with the notable exception of §3.1), but rather, becomes doubly-tokenized, still identical immediately following the doubling, followed by divergent evolution of the two minds immediately thereafter (or whenever consciousness is recommenced). If we wanted a precise term for this process we would call it *instantiate-new-identical-brain-state-token-(implicitly-referencing-same-mind-state-type-as-original)-then-dynamically-evolve-both-tokens-to-next-brain-states-and-continue*, but boiling this insufferable phrase down as a *split* is a remarkably convenient short-hand.

Some readers might propose that the use of the terms *splitting* or *doubling-then-diverging* is mere word play around the more basic concept of simply *copying*. There are two reasons the term *split* is more appropriate than *copy* or *duplicate*. First, *copy* is loaded with asymmetrical values. *Originals* are more proper, more valid, more bonafide, more genuine. *Copies* are, almost by definition, inferior, not only in potential physical state but in our assignment of primacy (ownership of the one true mind). These are the very connotations I wish to avoid.

There is a deeper reason *split* is a better term than *copy*, however. We simply and utterly cannot copy a type, and both minds and mind-states are types. Types only exist once (in a completely nonspatio-temporal way of course). A mind (a unique sequence of mind-states) cannot be copied because copying a type is fundamentally precluded by the underlying metaphysics. What we can do, however, is reference the mind multiple times from multiple occurrences—and those occurrences' temporal sequences of mind-states may then be said to *split* into separate sequences.

But surely we have copied something in an uploading procedure. Yes we have: the occurrences, most importantly the actual tokens (i.e., physical objects). To copy a token is to instantiate a second token of a physical configuration suitably identical within the required structural properties of the type it instantiates (and those structural properties can be quite broad; just consider the array of hand-writings and typefaces with which we can create '5' tokens to instantiate the '5' numeral type, to say nothing of nonArabic representations such as Mayan and Roman numerals, Morse code, semaphore, Braille, ASCII, etc. (see figure 5); a similar generality may very well apply to brains and minds). As I have argued, the physical configuration of an object is literally the information that it embeds at the level of abstraction appropriate to the type under consideration, so copying a token is tantamount to instantiating a second reference to the information that the token embeds, namely the bit string that describes the token.

So we can copy a token, but we cannot copy the type it refers to. Rhetorically, if new tokens (of like type) actually embedded new identical types, then the entire type/token framework would collapse. To even insinuate that types can be copied or duplicated is to imply that they can exist twice, and to suggest type multi-existence violates the most basic notion of what a type is in the first place. For this reason, I prefer the term *split*.

This concludes the presentation of my particular metaphysics of brain and mind. Next, I explore topics such as dualism and consciousness, including emergence and zombies. After those curious digressions, I formally state the primary argument of this book pertaining to the equality of various minds in uploading scenarios. From there we move on to other topics in the remaining chapters, such as free-will, and finally, an interpretation of the taxonomy through the lens of the metaphysics I have offered.

~ **6** ~

Debating Dualism
and Considering Consciousness

This chapter is divided into two major sections. In the first section I offer my thoughts on how the accusation of dualism is wielded as a rather clumsy sword in debates over the issues under consideration here. In the second section I tackle the potential concern that when interpreting an uploading scenario's success with respect to transferring, copying, or splitting a mind, there might be a fundamental difference in interpretive conclusion if we trade out the word *mind* for the word *consciousness*. I also briefly explore a few other concepts related to consciousness, mostly for the pure fun of the topic.

Dualism

Dualism isn't what it used to be. In its earlier and simpler presentations, primarily those of Descartes[18], it was quite straightforward, a supernatural essence which paired up with the brain to create the mind (through the pineal gland in the dead center of the brain no less, how splendidly specific). Naturally, Cartesian dualism is often seen quite favorably by religious believers since it aligns so nicely with the concept of a *soul*. For essentially the same reason, Cartesian dualism is re-

---

[18] Admittedly, dualism goes back as far as Plato, but Descartes is a reasonable point of embarkation too.

garded with little disagreement as being incompatible with materialistic philosophies of mind (to say nothing of being demonstrably incompatible with physics as the impact of a spiritual essence upon neural activity implies a form of perpetual motion [13]). However, dualism has diversified with astounding resilience to accommodate more materialistic views, so widely in fact that it seems to pull the most innocuous philosophies under its wing. Consequently, perspectives on mind that are unquestionably materialist and adherent to science are often branded as dualistic—and then summarily dismissed on that basis.

It is important to emphasize that some forms of dualism, subtle though they may be, are nevertheless entirely compatible with physicalism, materialism, and more importantly, science. David Chalmers openly admits that his theories and perspectives could be called *naturalistic dualism*, his own coinage [7], although his views have also been simply associated with more conventional *property dualism* (defined below). Pointedly, in the same article in which he presented naturalistic dualism, Chalmers labored to maintain a strict adherence to a materialistic and physical nature, but my primary concern is that such subtleties may be lost on some readers. Dualism can suffer from reflexive disregard in debates, depending on the willingness—or lack thereof—of detractors to tolerate the materialistic-compatible variants, such as property dualism, which while maintaining that matter and mind are fundamentally different kinds of things (philosophers refer to this as an *ontological* difference), nevertheless adheres to the view that mental states derive exclusively from physical phenomena by rational functionalist means. Property dualism also includes *emergent materialism* (my personal preference I wholly admit), which entails the innate emergence of mental phenomena from sufficiently complex and appropriately arranged complex systems, such as brains.

In attempting to determine whether my views fall under the rubric of some sort of dualism, the first observation is that the Library of Anaxagoras can, at a glance, appear to be rather dualistic. To propose that nonphysical entities (what I have consistently referred to via the classical terminology of Platonic *types* and *abstract occurrences*) can have an existence in their own right, separate from their physical associations, that they might even be organized into a space of related types (mind-state space, aka, the library) seems fairly dualistic. However, I find such broad usage of dualistic labeling to be stretching so far as to dispose of any meaning the concept might convey. We all happily use quasi-dualistic terminology in precisely this fashion. Why even have two words, brain and mind, unless we truly intend to use them to refer to different concepts? The mere recognition that there are disparate concepts at play here is not sufficient to assign dualism in my opinion. Surely the opponents of even this all-encompassing application of the term don't mean to imply the apparent opposite, that we should be barred from using the word *mind* and that it should be removed from our dictionaries on the claim that *it means the same thing as brain*[19]. They can't possibly mean that! We are then left with deciding for or against a dualism label based on the *relationship* between these concepts, all the while respecting that they are definitely both actual concepts! It might seem ridiculous to have to press this point, but for the experiences I have had in multiple discussions and debates in which the dualism accusation is used with positively cavalier abandon.

I can't give the nuances of dualistic debate a sufficient presentation in this book. It would, of course, involve teasing apart the numerous kinds of monism, dualism, pluralism, etc., and covering the distinctions separating various purported dualisms from purported nondualisms. That would be a huge book. One must truly delve into this quagmire to appreciate how tarred up the whole mess really is; there simply isn't enough room here to give it a proper presentation. The list of topics includes property dualism, predicate dualism, anomalous monism, neutral monism, functionalism, behavioralism, materialism, emergent materialism, reductive materialism, elimitive materialism, nonreductive physicalism, type physicalism, token physicalism, epiphenomenalism, panpsychism, biological naturalism, identity theory, multiple realizability—the list goes on and on. Furthermore, there don't appear to be particularly sharp boundaries between some of these ideas; there are debates not only over which of these philosophies is

---

[19] Searle would appear to agree with my repeated claims that vocabulary is a significant roadblock to understanding and communicating about these issues [42].

true, but also over which ones are compatible with other ones, which ones are subsets of other ones, which ones implicitly disprove other ones, etc. Venture forth at your own peril.

All that said, I am willing to admit to the modern and scientifically tenable notions of dualism, but only with great reservation. The mere whiff of dualism frequently undermines otherwise civil discourse by branding the identified dualist as readily dismissible (on the grounds of misapplied Cartesian absurdity). I have experienced this firsthand multiple times, seeing my ideas maligned not on the basis of topical analysis, but rather from a categorical accusation of broad-spectrum dualism. This is, in fact, the central problem concerning *pattern identity theory*, that it triggers immediate and unjustified accusations of overarching dualism with no consideration to the diverse fauna that modern dualism encompasses. The grand irony of such dualistic accusations is that in the next section I will interpret the ideas presented in this book as primarily monist, i.e., claiming that reality is of a single (physical) substance and that more abstract metaphysical considerations do not constitute a different kind of fundamental substance. These sorts of problems perfectly underline why I am uncomfortable with even the most conservative dualistic stance; many people are obstinate, not to the ideas, but to the term itself, subtleties be damned.

Consciousness

On one hand, I really didn't want to go within ten miles of consciousness in this book. There can't be a faster way to raise hackles than to offer one's personal take on the nature of consciousness, simply because both the diversity of opinions, and the conviction with which people hold those opinions, pretty much guarantee that I (and all other authors) will find few friends in the audience. On the other hand, consciousness is just positively *fun*, which will become obvious as we consider ideas including suicidal ants, sky-blackening flocks of birds, and of course, zombies. Reason enough to peek under the lid, I would say.

In this section, I want to get at the popular concern in mind-uploading speculation about whether a proposed procedure would preserve the subject's *consciousness* as opposed to any other related term (mind, identity, self, personhood, etc.), i.e., whether the consciousness successfully *transfers*, or rather, merely spawns a duplicate consciousness (or multiple such in the case of multi-uploads) while leaving the original untouched. To be clear, I am discussing what is often described as *the hard problem* of consciousness, what Chalmers describes as *experience* [7]: the intangible over-arching sense of our own existence, the feeling and qualia of our moment to moment circumstances, aka definition number three in the glossary (although I confess that in the glossary I essentially duck the question and defer to popular authorities [7, 13, 30, 41]).

Some readers may feel that in my presentation with respect to *minds*, I have already covered the issue of when an upload should be deemed successful—both in earlier sections and more importantly, although yet to come, in the next section (which brings this book to its final implications). I would essentially agree with such views. However, other readers may have skimmed over my copious attention to *mind*, hanging in suspense for the part where I finally address the delectable topic of consciousness. I hope to explicitly associate the two concepts as being equivalent in as far as mind-uploading interpretation is concerned. My argument to that effect is rather brief, to be presented shortly, and consequently much of this section meanders through issues of consciousness primarily as topics of interest in their own right, but not necessarily of deep relevance to the uploading question.

I prefer to avoid consciousness in most discussions and debates, favoring *minds* as the primary topic of consideration. This approach is defensible due to their shared locality: minds exhibit consciousness and consciousness is a characteristic of minds, so they literally colocate. This realization allows us to interchange the two terms in debates concerning whether either concept successfully *transfers* in a particular uploading scenario. If consciousness *transferred*, then so did the mind. If it failed to transfer, resulting in some manner of duplicate consciousness, then the same fate befell the mind. Due to this colocality, any qualitative judgement of an uploading scenario focusing on the resulting minds implicitly examines the associated consciousnesses in the same breath, and therefore the latter can be dispensed with, and thankfully so, due to its veritable ungraspableness.

If the proposed near-equivalence between mind and consciousness strikes the reader as inaccurate, then consider the hypothetical contrary position, a reductio ad absurdum in effect: that they are meaningfully distinct *in the context of judging mind-uploading success,* which is the only context of relevance to this discussion. To do so, there must be a scenario from the taxonomy in which one would conclude that the original mind has successfully *transferred* to the uploaded brain but the original consciousness has not—or vice versa. I suspect that interpretations to that effect are essentially nonexistent, and that is precisely why I believe we can reduce them to a single term for the duration of mind-uploading analysis.

However, despite the near perfect correspondence in when and where these concepts occur, they do describe (or at least evoke) dissimilar ideas and therefore are worth some brief disambiguation, even if only because these topics are so fascinating. Toward the end of this section, I will show that there is some loose relevance in the specific matter of consciousness and mind-uploading, thereby hopefully justifying the following digression.

Three Bugs

Before exploring the issue head-on, let's consider some curious cases, mostly because I find them so fascinating. In some sense, consciousness is best defined by what it is not. Insects offer some spectacular examples, perhaps because it violates our notions of what animals are that *any* kind of animal should exhibit a level of consciousness approximating that of a waffle iron. The following examples illuminate situations in which there is practically no *awareness* of one's circumstances.

To begin, there is the widely recognized example of the digger wasp (multiple species) that paralyzes and drags its prey to a nest (a tiny burrow into the ground), leaves the prey near the opening to briefly inspect the nest, remerges, and finally drags the prey inside to its eventual fate, which is shudderingly dreadful: when the wasp's eggs hatch, the larvae eat the supplied prey, which is still alive and therefore fresh, yet still paralyzed (and in the case of a related family of wasps, even eaten from the inside out!). However, if, while the wasp is down below, an experimenter moves the prey a few inches away, the wasp then, upon remerging, seems to reset its internal behavioral program. It drags the prey back to the nest, and then once again investigates the burrow even though it already did so only a moment ago. This sequence has been repeated by experimenters up to forty times with the wasp never figuring out what's going on [11, 12]. Natural selection never had to solve this problem because no naturally-occurring circumstances would conspire to mock the wasp so.

Another example is an *ant mill*, observed in army ants, in which a large number of foragers fall into a circular march, each ant following the ants ahead of it. Such circles can persist for hours or days until the ants incrementally collapse and die. Discovered in nature [3, 22, 39], this phenomenon has also been reproduced in laboratories [22] and computer simulations, including my own such simulations (see figure 11).

Finally, I recall seeing a video of a katydid or cricket lying on its back and perpetually spinning a foam peanut in its legs, which was suspended in the air above itself [37] (see figure 12). Such behavior might simply seem tedious, and not necessarily unconscious, except for the realization that the animal sincerely appeared to be *walking* along the piece of foam. In all likelihood, this poor creature believed (if that is the right word) that it was making steady forward progress along the underside of some surface—albeit upside down—all the while going absolutely nowhere with no presence of mind to its unfortunate predicament[20]. The video's description claimed that this behavior persisted for more than three hours.

---

[20] Others have noted that a mind-bending perspective on this situation is that the katydid is repeatedly circling a very very tiny planet while carrying the entire Earth on its back.

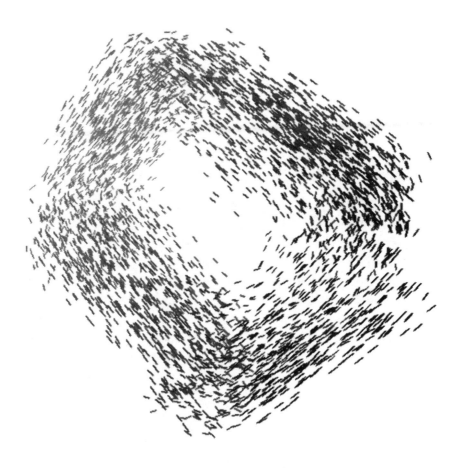

Figure 11. Computer simulation of an ant mill – This figure shows an *ant mill* from my artificial life program *Gnat Cloud* [50]. Although the program was not originally intended to produce ant mills (it is simply a fairly typical *flocking* simulation, which is a popular area of study within the field of artificial life), the ant mill emerged on its on as a result of the natural dynamics of the simulation's flocking rules. Such serendipitous surprises are most welcome and gratifying in artificial life studies.

Figure 12. Katydid with confused sense of locomotion – This figure shows a katydid or cricket in a pitiful state of confusion about its circumstances. In the associated video, this poor creature is seen spinning this foam peanut in its legs for hours on end, clearly under the impression that it is walking along the underside of a branch or related structure. Not only does the katydid lack the necessary consciousness to quickly resolve the falsehood of its predicament (which is forgivable as a potentially *aliased* sensory experience), but more seriously, it lacks the longer-term awareness that, over time, it is clearly not going anywhere.

What these examples demonstrate is animals in a state of painfully unconscious behavior (fatally so). Not only are they likely unconscious of their immediate actions à la definition two in the glossary (is the katydid really *thinking* about walking?) but more seriously they are utterly oblivious to their larger circumstances and therefore unable to correct their error. R. Wiley could describe these situations by observing that they are receivers of environmental signals which instantiate and modify internal mental states (that is to say that such signals are *received*) but that these poor insects lack any introspection into their own internal mental states [54]. The larger point isn't that we should expect similarly obstinate behavior from brainier animals, such as mammals and birds. Rather, the point is that we can clearly observe animal behavior which is dumbfoundingly unconscious. If we can, at least in part, define consciousness by what it is *not*, then it is a worldly- and self-awareness that explicitly alleviates the sorts of incognizance shown above. The insect examples are easy to interpret precisely because they are so transparently unconscious. The immediate question is then: where do we draw the line? Should we grant consciousness to bower birds and beavers in the frenzy of construction? Or, should we dispense with a cutoff and consider a consciousness spectrum? (And if so, do all humans reside at the same point at all times? And is it an extreme point that cannot be theoretically surpassed?) These are all open questions.

The insect examples just presented may somewhat entangle the second and third definitions of consciousness offered in the glossary, namely momentary awareness of one's immediate actions and the grander awareness of one as a cognitive self, or the experiencing of one's own cognition. More to the point, the further toward the hard problem we get, toward true human-like consciousness as we conceive the notion, the more intangible the idea becomes (quickly entering the realm of qualia, the unique feeling of a sensation like color or taste, surely as thorny a topic as there ever was) while at the same time the more resistant to external objective verification it becomes. Being truly subjective in nature, we really can never know whether other animals are conscious in this grander fashion—or artificial intelligence—or even other people for that matter, this last point being central to solipsistic philosophy[21]. That is why my consideration of consciousness veers toward the glossary's second definition, that of our momentary awareness of particular activities, as shown in the examples provided above.

Emergence

Moving on from curiously obtuse insects, we can tackle consciousness more directly. Although the literature is replete with expositions on consciousness, I would suggest the reader check out Chalmers' article *Facing Up to the Problem of Consciousness* [7], not to be confused with his much longer book from the same time period. The paper is accessibly brief and sets the stage for debates that continued for years after publication, regardless of whether one ultimately agrees with him. Classically, consciousness has been associated with the notion of awareness, especially *self-awareness*, which has been described as a signal receiver's awareness of its own internal altered states in response to various signals [54]. Chalmers prefers to conceptualize consciousness not by the common moniker of awareness but rather as *experience*: to experience a mental state is to be conscious. Chalmers has considered numerous neurophysiological theories of consciousness and across the board has drawn a similar conclusion, namely that they do more to explain the possible physical causes of mental states associated with consciousness, but never the reason for why (or how) such mental states yield visceral experience. As one example among many, he points out Crick and Koch's theory of 35–75 Hz neural oscillations as a basis for—or at least a neural correlate to—consciousness. Chalmers simply concludes: but why should such oscillations produce *experience*? His primary point is that we don't just need to discover *which* brain functions and activity cause consciousness, but *why* and *how* they do so, and on that point he finds existing theories lacking.

---

[21] A fascinating tangent suggested by R. Wiley is that if we conceive of consciousness as awareness of one's internal state changes in response to received signals, and if we take into consideration the noise inherent in such signals and communication, *including* the noise in our own perception of and report about our own internal states, then we might actually form erroneous beliefs about our own consciousness [54]! R. Wiley's entire book is dedicated to the implications of such noise in all manner of signals as conveyed and received by various interacting agents.

There are many proposed solutions to the hard problem of consciousness. My preferred stance feels extremely right to me—a claim that is certainly true of everyone else as well. For me, consciousness is, for admittedly currently unknown reasons, a natural emergent consequence of the dynamic evolution of certain arrangements of matter, namely the sort found in human brains. I admit this broad generalization would apply to most people's viewpoint in modern times. However, I would further propose that not only might consciousness be *the consequence* of such activity, but might better be conceptualized as directly being synonymous with such activity. That is to say, I theorize that the coordinated behavior of the brain might simply *be* consciousness. I like to phrase it this way because it prevents us from separating conceivably inseparable concepts. If A produces or causes or gives rise to B, or if B emerges or arises from A, or any number of similarly sounding descriptions, then we can wantonly imagine A without B, which is a very important idea to Chalmers (this idea underlies his entire theory in fact, evidenced by his primary thought experiment of imagining people without consciousness, i.e., zombies, to be presented below). Alternatively, if A and B are simply different levels of abstraction, or different *ways of viewing,* the same essential thing, then we are saved from what might be a fundamental conceptual error. John Searle has expressed similar concerns in his attempts to clarify his stance on property dualism. In his case, he dislikes the description that consciousness *arises* from the brain and prefers to describe it as a state that a brain can be in [42], specifically to alleviate the otherwise overly tempting separation of brain and mind. I prefer my wording, less a *state* (although I appreciate Searle's point), and more simply the confluence of global neural functionality. To understand my perspective, consider that we don't say the coordinated flight of a group of birds *causes* flocking (or even that flocking *arises* from coordinated flight, or even that flocking is a *state* that a group of birds can be in, although both of these alternatives feel closer than the causal terminology). No, we simply say coordinated flight *is* flocking. It almost isn't correct to say that flocking is a causal consequence of coordinated flight so much as *being* coordinated flight[22]. I conceptualize consciousness with respect to brain activity in a similar manner. Notice that I am focusing, not on the parts (the birds or neurons) or even the confluent noun (the group of birds[23] or the brain), but rather on the verb: the act of flocking or *consciousating* (since no verb exists in our language for this concept). The crucial concept is the *behavior* of these systems: legs aren't running, running is what legs do. Flocking is what groups of birds in flight do. Consciousness is what certain arrangements of neurons *do*. Why, you ask? If you find the question of *why* absurd with respect to birds (why is coordinated flight *flocking* per se?), then my argument is that we must equally drop it with respect to brains. *Whyness* just doesn't enter.

In the previous section I claimed that I would present my ideas as less dualistic and more monistic. The conceptualization presented in the previous paragraph emphasizes my point on this matter. Not only am I claiming, contrary to all but the most liberal of dualistic notions, that mind is not a radically different metaphysical substance from brain, but rather merely a quantification of the information embedded within the brain's physical structure, but furthermore, I claim that mental processes are not derived *from* neurological processes but rather are

---

[22] The closest I have ever come to what I believe it would be like to witness consciousness as an external observer is the tear-jerking beauty, complexity, and richness of massive flocks (dare I say swarms) of swallows and starlings roosting [2] (such flocks are called *murmurations* of starlings and *flights* of swallows). Many excellent videos can be found online in addition to the provided citation. To understand what such complex dynamic systems look like, what patterns they are capable of, what their dynamic evolution truly involves, one simply must witness it in action, either in person or in video; textual descriptions and photographs are entirely incapable of conveying the concept, which is essentially my point (see main text). When I view such massive flocks, I feel like I am looking into a system closer to revealed consciousness than any other system so easily exposed to our senses. I must confess, the first time I witnessed it was as religious an experience as I have ever personally had. To be clear, I'm not remotely saying that flocks of birds actually *are* conscious and any quote to that effect would be dishonestly misrepresentative. I am saying that this one example comes closer than other I can conceive to illustrating what it might be like (analogously, not identically) to witness another person's consciousness *from the outside*, i.e., by observing their brain's physical activity.

[23] We must be careful with our terminology. The word *flock* is used as a noun to merely refer to a group of birds (even with specialized terms for specific species, as noted in footnote 22) and as a verb to describe a completely different idea: a specific mode of coordinated action, a concept that is not remotely captured by the noun version. If I were to use the word *flock* as a noun where this footnote appears, it would confuse this matter.

a way of summarizing those processes outright. That was the point of the previous paragraph and that is precisely the way in which I interpret my metaphysics as essentially nondualistic, almost to the point of full-blown monism. I'm sure many philosophers will disagree with me on this analysis, but this feels sensible to me.

Chalmers' initial response to my theory would probably be similar to his response to other theories: why should coordinated brain activity give rise to experience—but that response would fail to comprehend the true depth of my argument. I would not agree to the description that experience *arises* secondarily from brain activity, thereby requiring an additional explanation. I would say consciousness *directly is* what brain activity evokes as conceptualized *from the inside*. In the previous sentence, I would like to have said that consciousness is what certain brain activity *feels like from the inside* but that phrasing would confuse matters by suggesting some additional agent must be doing the feeling (the homunculus interpretation, as Dennett describes it in his notion of a *Cartesian theater* [13]). This is not my point at all, so I simply say such activity evokes consciousness from an internal perspective. The question of who is doing the feeling is answered by *the overall system itself*. To be a brain in a state of such activity literally is to be conscious, full stop. There is no room for a subsequent question of how experience, as a secondary effect, remains to arise for it is not secondary to begin with; it is directly established within the associated brain activity. The analogy of flocking is one way to interpret my meaning on this issue: once a group of birds has *flocked*, there is no more causal investigation of flocking to be done. From *the inside*, the flock has commenced its own flocking, the brain has commenced its own consciousness vis-a-vis its various activity. Related analogies could be offered but they would be similar in flavor: they would describe a system in which the concept in question is a verb as opposed to a noun, namely the activity of some massively coordinated network.

One challenge I believe Chalmers would raise (because he anticipates, and attempts to dismantle, emergence in his book) is that there is an additional experiential quality to consciousness that remains to be explained, whereas in my favorite analogy of flocking, there is purportedly no additional metaphysical property to consider once the under-lying physical mechanisms have been analyzed. I can't overemphasize how deeply I disagree with this argument. We absolutely cannot know what sort of additional metaphysical properties may accompany flock-ing or other complex systems, even in materialistically entailed ways. We know, for an absolute fact, that certain complex physical systems can invoke seemingly mysterious metaphysical phenomena, for that is the brain/mind relationship at the heart of these considerations. There-fore, we should, if we would be rationally minded, be open to the idea that other complex systems can involve other sorts of metaphysics. By definition, we couldn't probe the extra properties of flocks if they did exist, so Chalmers is wrong to confidently declare them nonexistent; he can't know that! This is Chalmers' entire point with respect to brains. He would claim that one would never predict, by studying a brain, that its processes involve consciousness (I'm admittedly undecided whether I agree with this sentiment). This position is central to his thesis, but he fails to realize how this logic must extend to other complex systems. Don't misunderstand me on this. I am not remotely proposing that flocks of birds contain the exact same metaphysical property we know as consciousness. Such a claim would be tantamount to *panpsychism* (the idea that consciousness pervades the physical universe), and I see no value in such notions. I am saying that if there were *any other* sort of abstract metaphysical property at all at play in, say, flocks of birds or ecosystems or properly configured computer networks, then by Chalmers' own logic, there would be *absolutely no way* for us to detect them, so Chalmers is categorically wrong to dismiss them and conclude that brains necessarily involve an additional level of property in a way that flocks definitely lack; we can't logically make that claim. I believe that the higher phenomena that instantiate along with complex neural activity[24] are simply intrinsic to the behavior of such systems, and for all we know there could be an infinitude of unknowable metaphysical phenomena that essentially represent the confluent functionality of other complex systems.

---

[24] You can sense in my writing how desperate I am to contort our linguistic limitations to avoid anachronisms like *cause, arise,* etc.

This has been the best I can offer at the current time as to how my theory of consciousness works. I sincerely hope that future advances in neuroscience will clarify these issues—and of course it is my prediction that such advances will, at least in part, support this theory (for otherwise I would not hold such a theory in the first place).

Zombies

A *philosophical zombie* (or p-zombie) is a hypothetical proposal designed to question our intuitions and expectations about the relationship between brains and consciousness. The p-zombie is a very specific idea that bears practically no resemblance to conventional zombies, either Hollywood or Haitian. It looks and acts exactly like a normal person but contains no internal consciousness. A zombie doesn't experience qualia (the feeling of the redness of red or the painfulness of pain), but acts precisely as if it had perceived these sensations. An injured zombie cries out, yet experiences nothing. Notably, it doesn't run on a *simpler* brain that *cheats* the appearance of natural external behavior, since simplified hardware could be identified via surgical or post-mortem dissection, which is incompatible with the zombie thought experiment. No, a zombie is, by the terms of the proposal, molecularly and functionally identical to a human, yet for whatever reason lacks all internal awareness, consciousness, experience, etc. By definition, there is no objective way to tell if someone is a zombie. Anyone in the world (or *everyone* in the world) might actually be a p-zombie with the single exception of yourself—and of course anyone else can make the same claim, thus rendering *you* a zombie from their POV. In other words, I may have written this book for a world full of unconscious automatons.

Zombies received a significant boost when Chalmers presented and argued for them in the mid-nineties [8], which sparked notable debate at the time. It remains undetermined whether zombies *make sense*. Chalmers would argue that they make logical sense even if they don't represent reality, while others, such as Dennett and Searle, have argued that zombies are in fact logically inconsistent [13, 41].

My take on zombies aligns closely with the philosophical positions of physicalism and emergentism, namely that they are intrinsically inconsistent. Admittedly, physicalist arguments are only persuasive to those of a physicalist inclination to begin with. That said, in my view, the neural processing that a zombie will perform (such neural processing is required of the zombie theory since on a physical level they are indistinguishable from humans) will, ipso facto, give rise to consciousness, just as it does in nonzombies. For reasons currently unknown, such emergent phenomena are apparently intrinsic to certain forms of complex functionality and network behavior, such as exhibited by brains. Given identical kinds of neural function, a zombie's brain must necessarily yield identical kinds of emergent mental experience. Therefore, any purported zombie will implicitly experience consciousness and thereby immediately cease to be a zombie, thus rendering the thought experiment paradoxical. The entire idea simply collapses under this particular interpretation.

My view is all but identical to that of both Dennett and Searle (though I must claim credit for devising it on my own, just as many societally invisible philosophers can rightly claim they are entitled to *credit* for their own ideas). Searle argues that zombies are impossible in the case of biologically identical copies since consciousness simply must emerge from such substrate, as we are well aware it apparently does [41], even if we don't yet understand why or how. This is essentially the argument I just laid out. Where Searle and I part ways is his bizarre dismissal that comparable structural arrangements, but of other material kinds, otherwise performing identical functionality above a reasonable level of abstraction, would not necessarily be conscious for precisely the same reason as in the biological case[25]. Why Searle is so biocentric is not remotely clear to me.

---

[25] Searle is difficult to comprehend on this issue. On one hand, he states that he could imagine (or permit) artificial consciousness. On the other hand, he repeatedly describes consciousness as a conspicuously *biological* phenomenon, and has virtually defined his career by excluding computational means to that end. Furthermore, he has stated outright that, in his view, neurons are not merely *"neural computers"* [41]. Hence, he would presumably reject a confluence of such devices, i.e., a type-2 brain as defined in the glossary. But if he would reject a system as closely analogous to a biological brain as the type-2 model, then what sort of artificial brain is he claiming to be open-minded about in the first place? Frankly, I am not sure what he is claiming on this issue.

As noted, Chalmers and supporters would be quick to disagree with me, to say nothing of disagreeing with the likes of Dennett and Searle, but I take some solace in the fact that even among the cognoscente there are plenty who mostly agree with me. I don't have room to give the field its full consideration here, of course. Suffice it to say, the literature is replete on this topic should the reader be curious. All that said, in this brief account, I merely wish to present the idea and my particular interpretation.

Philosophical musing about p-zombies seems relatively derailed from the mind-uploading debate, except that it can occasionally crop up. Most of the time detractors grant consciousness to uploads and merely argue that their consciousness is not that of the original subject, but some detractors might offer a stronger claim, that uploads utterly lack consciousness and are mere automatons, that they are essentially zombies. If valid, this charge would be a severe argument against mind-uploading, not only in principle, but also as policy. Merely arguing for a new consciousness only denies biological humans the opportunity to upload, while arguing that uploading represents a more fundamental failure, namely failing to produce *any* consciousness, proposes that should humanity undertake the process on a large scale, we would march not only to our individual deaths, but also to our species' extinction. Gravitational concerns if ever there were.

Conclusion

As I argued at the beginning of this section, speculation about consciousness is, on some level, tangential to the uploading question since it can probably be addressed more directly by considering minds instead. Unless, during various considerations of uploading, there is a *meaningful* distinction between mind and consciousness specifically relevant to that context's particular debate, I would urge simply considering the status of the various minds and avoiding consciousness. Specifically, unless there are scenarios in the taxonomy which interpret the fate of the associated minds and consciousnesses differently, then there is no need to investigate both separately.

~ 7 ~

Equality of
Post-Upload-Procedure Minds

In this chapter I bring the book to its climactic argument, and yet, despite the preeminence of this chapter's purpose and conclusion, it is relatively short. The reasoning is fairly straightforward: the book up to this point has essentially derived my final argument without even having to state it. I see this as a good thing. If an argument need be further advanced after all the evidence is presented, then something was lacking in the initial presentation. Alternatively, if the conclusions of the presentation of the evidence are complete and consistent, then actually stating the final argument is practically redundant—but such finality is a practical necessity, so here we go.

I have described how a mind can conceptually split as a result of an uploading procedure. Where once there was one mind, there are now two (or more), by which I really mean, where once there was a single occurrence of a mind-state type, there are now two occurrences of the same mind-state type, along with two tokens of the corresponding brain-state type, which will then go off in different directions through mind-state space and brain-state space. To be precise, splitting is a two-step process, both doubling and divergence. The divergence occurs following the doubling at the next *dynamic* moment, namely when the two tokens (brains) evolve to two inherently different brain-states and take their associated mind-state sequences (minds) off in different directions. If the upload procedure is conscious in nature, then the divergence occurs instantaneously, whereas if the procedure is unconscious, then it won't actually occur until the two new minds awaken, which could be thousands of years. My preferred term of a *split* represents the overall process of both doubling and dynamically diverging—which as just stated, may take a long time to complete.

To be absolutely clear on how this theory assigns identity, the new minds gain autonomy and independent identity the instant their dynamic processes diverge in state. They are in absolutely no way *the same person* after that moment, and both speculation and accusation to that effect are off the table. I would hope that emphasizing this point isn't necessary, but I prefer to avoid confusion on the matter.

The preeminent argument of this book is that the two minds resulting from a typical scan-and-copy procedure are truly equal in the primacy of their claim to the identity of *the* original mind. I claim that the mind in the original biological brain is no more entitled to primacy than the mind in the upload. This can be a rather startling claim and a difficult philosophical position to hold, for we can consider a challenging scenario in which the biological brain and mind do not even *realize* that the procedure has occurred. Even under such circumstances, I would still claim that the mind has evenly *split* in two, with one descendant associated with the biological brain and one with the upload, but with both having absolutely equal primacy to the original mind.

Although this claim seems initially astounding, I would hope to show how we can comprehend the scenario from both minds' respective POVs and thereby grant them equal validity. We instinctively interpret these sorts of thought experiments from the POV of the original biological brain and the mind that rides along with it, but I consider that to be a logical error. We should be just as willing to view the scenario through the eyes of the uploaded mind. Take a moment and try to really internalize this argument, don't just understand it as an objective statement and then summarily dismiss it. Try to hold onto this idea briefly, for it can profoundly change how you conceive of what a mind actually is and what it feels like to be a mind, and I consider that to be a worthy revelation. While this style of argument is an appeal to emotion and qualitative feeling, it floats atop the more structured metaphysical theory I have heretofore presented. We can use the metaphysics of types and occurrences to guide our interpretation of the thought experiment such that we are less prone to otherwise innate prejudices. That is what the metaphysical aspect of the issue buys us, the strength to dismiss otherwise difficult prejudices in perspective.

Many readers will nevertheless utterly balk at this argument. After all, perhaps you, the reader, were just uploaded a moment ago without the slightest awareness on your part. Surely, as the biological *original*, you may consider yourself the primary owner of the identity, and the upload, wherever it may reside, as a humble facsimile. To best understand, or better yet to *feel*, the counter-argument, consider that perhaps you were just uploaded as described, but *you are the upload* and someone else is the original, despite your having no awareness of the procedure and despite holding an unquestionable conviction as to your identity. Although this is a more difficult angle on the scenario, since your surroundings didn't suddenly change, it was previously shown that our visual experience is not physically required (by any fundamental rules of nature) to be consistent from one moment to the next. Therefore, you could suddenly upload, and actually be the upload, in a different body, brain, and location, but be presented with an identical visual stimulus. Although technically more challenging, this scenario is not precluded by the laws of nature, which leaves us contemplating it from both POVs. If you just uploaded in the midst of reading this paragraph, none the wiser of it, and you are the true original, then your feeling of primacy is justified on conventional grounds. But if the same situation occurred and you are the upload, your primacy is still equally justified. The only alternative is to willfully dismiss your own identity!

If we take the salient properties of a mind to be its unassailably nonspatial and nonphysical cognitive aspects (its function, behavior, experience, feelings—its subjective perspective), and not its physical aspects (its brain and/or structure), and more importantly, if we interpret the application of the *split* in the very precise metaphysical manner I have offered, then we must contend with the true equality (in primacy, not identity) of the two or more minds in question. The physical atoms comprising one brain or the other are piteously irrelevant to the grandeur of mind, and to favor one brain (and its embedding of a descendent mind) over the other brain (and its descendent mind) is difficult to reconcile within the theory presented here.

The point this chapter emphasizes is not the physical equality of the two brains (though identical they may be, or until they diverge), but more crucially, their equality in lineal descent from the ancestral mind: neither mind is *more* descendant from the original mind, or better identified as actually being the original mind itself. Their subjective perspectives are of equal validity when weighing their respective claims to *own* or embed the original mind's identity. Our language once again impels me to speak of *the* mind, as if there is one root mind at the core of our considerations. There is not. There is admittedly but a single mind that precedes the upload procedure, but there are two after it is complete, each with a valid POV, and with the two POVs being of equal balance—even if one is still housed in the biological brain! I have endeavored to convey this idea and hope I have reached at least a few readers. To those for whom this argument falls short, I thank you for considering it.

Some readers may take my description and still feel no compunction about assigning primacy to the older biological brain token. It is my hope that the theory presented here can help one understand why that perspective can be perceived as flawed. Our topic of interest is not atoms nor molecules, nor even cells nor computers. It is not structural continuity, nor is it spatial locality, nor lastly is it the *age* of a particular arrangement of atoms. In fact, our topic of interest is not a material entity at all, and likewise does not possess any property that might be assigned to a material entity.

We are interested in minds and the subjective perspectives they contain. Association with particular brains is incidental so long as brains refer to the same mind—and as soon as two brains diverge and refer to separate minds the split is fundamentally even, offering no primacy to either side. Minds are strictly nonspatio-temporal concepts. They are a type, namely a type of sequence of mind-state types, still nonspatio-temporal, but mind-states are isomorphic with brain-state types, and those can spatio-temporally occur (as a brain-state token, i.e., a brain at a given instant in time). It is through this indirect composition of types, abstract occurrences of types, and finally tokenized occurrences of types that we can associate minds with brains. This is how we relate one to the other in our thinking on this issue—but we must focus our analysis on minds, for that is where subjective perspective, sense of identity, and consciousness reside. In the next chapter, I offer a potentially novel theory of free-will. Following that, the final chapter considers how this conceptualization of mind informs us about the thought experiments in the taxonomy.

~ 8 ~

Free-Will and the
Temporal Anthropic Principle

This chapter presents what I believe to be a relatively novel theory concerning free-will. Ultimately, the question of free-will doesn't play a particularly important role in mind-uploading philosophy. (It affects general philosophy of mind of course, but has little to say specifically about the uploading question.) However, given that I think my perspective on free-will is relatively uncommon, and that, as will be revealed, the metaphysics I have offered can be interpreted as defending my perspective, I think the idea is worth a quick presentation.

There are multiple ways of tackling the question of free-will, both how to define it and how to analyze whether we legitimately possess it. With regard to the definition, I prefer the wording offered in the glossary, namely that minds can express true *choice* in the various situations they encounter. This is a radical simplification of the broader topic and the reader can find excellent surveys and arguments elsewhere [38, 40]. I will focus primarily on the *physically deterministic* issue, which asks whether the microscopic material and force interactions of the universe are perfectly predetermined by the laws of physics, and if so, how such a conclusion propagates to macroscopic phenomena and ultimately affects free-will. Note that one interesting intermediate interpretation permits physical reality to not be deterministic at the microscopic level, in that microscopic phenomena would not necessarily replicate identically if the timeline were *rerun*, but nevertheless that physical reality be

stochastic such that macroscopic phenomena are essentially deterministic at the level of macroscopic properties [40]. The way a gas diffuses
throughout a volume is a common example of such reasoning.

Other approaches to determinism, specifically with regard to free-
will, include *biological determinism* (genetic predetermination) and *psychological determinism* (our behavior is constrained by subconscious and
inescapable drives). Additionally, one might prefer *compatibilism*, which
attempts to accept full-blown physical determinism while still allowing
free-will. Needless to say, the literature is rich on this topic.

In the discussion below, I focus on conventional physical determinism, the notion that if the timeline were rerun from identical circumstances, then precisely identical events would transpire down to the
smallest detail. I approach the issue from this perspective primarily
because it is how people usually initially contemplate free-will and is
therefore accessible to the most readers. Furthermore, because my im-
minent theory should extend to other forms of determinism anyway, I
may as well tackle the lowest level. Note that it is fairly irrelevant
whether quantum mechanics ultimately precludes physical determinism (the jury appears to be out on this question [21]); it is nevertheless a
reasonable hypothetical scenario in which to offer my theory.

In my view, free-will neither exists nor doesn't exist, but rather is
a meaningless term, and weighing the two positions is a meaningless
question. I don't mean unimportant or uninteresting. I mean truly
meaningless. In some sense I am claiming that the issue of free-will is a
category error in that the presumed validity of the question is in fact
incorrect; it is *categorically* not a valid question to begin with.

The universe does not permit *running the tape over again*. If we
cannot run a scenario twice to observe potentially different choices or
their implications, then for all intents and purposes, there was always
only one path through time, the one that, in retrospect, prevailed in the
timeline. I call this the *Temporal Anthropic Principle*:

> **Temporal Anthropic Principle:** *We find ourselves within the
> occurring timeline precisely because it is the only timeline in
> which we could ever exist.*

This claim is not a rejection of either physical determinism or free-will, but rather a rejection of their conceptual validity. The claim that there could only ever be one timeline does not necessarily reject free-will because the future portion of the timeline nevertheless remains unwritten; it may or may not result from free-will. That said, looking backward from some yet unreached future time, there will only have ever been one path from now to then, the path that actually occurred. Likewise, looking backward from now to some past time, there was only way that the timeline could have gotten us from then to now, the way that did in fact occur.

Since we don't know what the timeline will ultimately be, we are perfectly entitled to assume that, and operate as if, we possess free-will entirely regardless of whether free-will is actually true or false. Curiously, this assumption terminologically presumes free-will: we can only *choose to operate as if we have free-will* if *we have free-will*.

So long as we can neither verify nor disprove free-will through repetitive experimentation (rerunning the tape), both realizations are essentially equivalent. Our reality (our universe) would not transpire any differently depending on whether or not free-will is true because it only gets one shot. To be fair, we can say that what *caused* the timeline to unroll as it did legitimately depends upon free-will's truthhood, but the transpiring of events themselves doesn't actually vary as a result of this distinction: if free-will is true, then a sequence of events results from conscious choices, and if free-will is false, then the exact same sequence of events transpires anyway, but not due to free-will—but the same events occur in either case! That is the crux of my point.

Recast in the metaphysics of this book, having defined a mind as a unique sequence of mind-states that, to a reasonable approximation, encapsulates the memories of one's life from birth (approximately) to the present, we can appreciate the following realization: you could only be the person who you presently are (i.e., a particular mind, a particular sequence of mind-states up to the current moment) in precisely one conceivable way, the way that you actually are. There is no other sequence of mind-states through mind-state space, no other confluence of memories, that could even remotely be identified as you.

The claim that you cannot exist in any other way is of course a restatement of the anthropic argument. The crucial point, regardless of free-will, is that in retrospect from any point in time, your mind (state sequence) can only have occurred as it actually has occurred, for to postulate otherwise is to say that you wouldn't exist.

This point is often overlooked in fanciful speculations about alternate timelines, parallel universes, etc. During such speculation we should summarily dismiss ourselves (and everyone else) as utterly dead, and should view the universe or reality under consideration as populated by an entirely unrelated people. To illustrate this point, consider how readily we patently reject any *sameness* of identity of an upload whose memories are, in fact, identical up to within fractions of a second following an upload procedure. The entire debate concerning uploading, over the success or failure to *transfer* a mind, hinges in part on absolutely minuscule differences in state (and in part on other considerations such as spatial and conscious continuity). Surely, if the mind of an upload in a nondestructive procedure, a mind with an identical ancestry to that of the original subject, is regarded as unambiguously unique in identity, i.e., as a wholly different person (note that the issue of assigning primacy of resulting minds relative to the original subject, or of judging the procedure's *successful mind transfer* is irrelevant to the current discussion; we are merely considering whether multiple independent minds can be considered *the same person* here), then we must absolutely reject the professed sameness of identity of a mind in an alternate timeline, in which the person in question isn't even as similar as an upload since he or she doesn't share identical memories with our current and actual selves!

Existentialism

The Temporal Anthropic Principle and its consequences for free-will should surely have implications for other areas of philosophy as well. For example, existentialism is often assumed to rely heavily upon free-will to power its humanistic self-determination. Jean-Paul Sartre's dictum that humanity is *"condemned to freedom"* [38] gives us a concise reduction of the (or a) core existentialist perspective, namely that we not only possess freedom (of choice, of action, of attitude) but that such freedom is less a gift than a curse, or that, at the very least, it is a cold fact with which we must contend day by day whether we like it or not. When Sartre says we are *"condemned,"* he is admitting the convenience of the lack of responsibility we would benefit from if we were not free; hence we are *condemned* to the responsibility that accompanies our apparent freedom. But are we actually free? Is that premise sound? That is where temporal anthropicism enters. Sartre's explanation for our freedom is that unlike certain simple objects, whose purpose predates their invention (e.g., a paper-cutter, his preferred example, must be conceived before it can be invented and built), humans come with no a priori purpose (and he resoundingly denies religious explanations to this quandary). In his own words, a paper-cutter's *"essence precedes its existence,"* and in our case the opposite is true: we exist first, with no purpose, and must then define our purpose (our essence) through our cognitive and active lives. Clearly, to engage in such self-definition we must have the *freedom* to do so, so free-will, not only in cognition but also in action, is fundamental to Sartre's existentialism. As we will see, temporal anthropicism may have some dire consequences for Sartre's vision of free-will.

Friedrich Nietzsche is certainly among the most prominent philosophers associated with existentialism (and therefore worth a brief comment here), although he predates the formality of the term. Nietzsche's body of work is so enormous that it is easy to find statements spread across his writing that are seemingly contradictory. On one hand, his *Overhuman* or *Superman*, described in *Thus Spoke Zarathustra* [33], represents an ideal to which he believes humanity should (or could) aspire in some far-flung future after we shed our amygdala-driven pre-history. One trait he specifically grants to a being as self-actualized as the overhuman is ultimate freedom, if not necessarily over unrelenting physical laws, then at least over the path and purpose of his life. Clearly, the overhuman requires free-will in order to operate. Yet, we can also see in Nietzsche a dismissal (if not denial) of free-will. In *Beyond Good and Evil*, he characterizes it as *"boorish simplicity"* [34], although in the very same sentence he rails equally against the opposing position of *"unfree-will,"* which he describes as *"cause and effect,"* clearly a nineteenth-century reference to physical determinism. All in all, Nietzsche's concerns on that matter strike me as more focused on the moral implications of the various perspectives, and less on the metaphysical implications—in my opinion. That said, he certainly believed that people should desire and seek self-determination, and such a notion is difficult to reconcile with full-blown physical determinism, so how might temporal anthropicism affect his ideas?

When weighing the impact of temporal anthropicism on existentialism or any other system with strong tendencies in favor of free-will, bear in mind that I would still permit the possibility of free-will's truthhood given an unwritten future, and therefore not necessarily claim to undermine the system. Rather, my point is that the entire topic of free-will is anthropically pointless. First, let us consider classical anthropicism, namely the perplexing life-friendly nature of our universe given a near-infinite variety of possible configurations that would be markedly deadlier, or rephrased: *"Don't tell me I can't live in a universe in which every single location is 10,000 degrees. That's my choice to make!"* Thus, classical anthropicism does appear to limit our freedom at least a little bit, such as the freedom to live in a ridiculously hot universe. To be fair, Sartre would quickly retort that we still posses the mental freedom to either accept that limitation or pout about it, and that perhaps that is the freedom he meant in the first place—and more to the point, he probably never intended to refer to our *physical* freedom beyond the reasonable circumstances of biological life support.

So, although there may be a limitation on our opportunities lurking in classical anthropicism, it doesn't appear to be *particularly* limiting, or by association, harmful to free-will, since the choices it limits are pretty silly, as just illustrated. It merely *condemns* us to live in a plausible universe, if one can consider that a condemnation at all; it hardly impinges our freedom to explore the possibilities of our nature, our humanity, our existentialist potential.

However, the argument is *much* worse in the case of temporal anthropocism. Classical anthropicism merely argues that life in general (any life, all life, life as a concept) should be found in universes that support the requirements of life. Alternatively, temporal anthropocism argues that *you as a particular person*, as a particular mind, are utterly constrained to your given life and no other. Even the slightest deviation from the one true timeline would obliterate us all from existence. Despite the popular recreation of speculating about alternative timelines, there's actually no conceivable notion as *living in an alternate timeline* or *your parallel self from another reality*. Such proposals are logical nonsense with respect to the way I have presented minds.

We could rephrase the earlier question: *"Don't tell me I couldn't possibly exist in a timeline in which Alexander marched all the way to the Pacific? Who are you to tell me what temporal history I am required to inherit?"* But actually, that is precisely my argument. Forget for the moment that if there were a sufficiently large change in the timeline, none of us would exist simply because the incomprehensible coincidence of our precise genetic confluence would never have occurred—and more so, that such genetic deviations would have manifested early on such that our entire ancestry going back millennia would never have lived (thereby proposing an entire planet and history peopled by a completely different population, and likewise in which not a single person we know of ever existed). That observation is not even my central point, relevant though it surely is. Rather, my point is that to possess the history and memory of such a variable timeline you can no longer be *you* (nor a *modified* or *similar* you, as explained below).

For the sake of argument, if we ignore the genetic reasoning just presented (and this really is truly inconceivable), then even if a genetic *you* existed in an alternative timeline, such a clone, possessing a different set of memories, would be an entirely different person, not similar, not *parallel*, but simply different, full stop. Although such a notion doesn't jive with our casual permissions on alternative timeline musing, it is, in fact, part and parcel with both popular interpretations of mind-uploading thought experiments and with the metaphysics I have presented. People (minds) of only the slightest variation in experience are readily assigned indisputably unique identity and personhood. To be from a different history, your mind must represent a different path through mind-state space, which makes it a definitively different mind with fully realized uniqueness of identity. That person cannot be identified as you for the same reason we feel so challenged by various uploading scenarios.

To illustrate this point, recognize that it is central to why we instinctively reject nondestructive teleportation (§2.2.1.1) on the interpretation that completing the procedure involves blatantly killing a distinct person (the original) who has essentially nothing in common with the resulting teleported person, identity-wise. Likewise, it is synonymous with why, short of the carefully prescribed interpretation of mind-splitting I have offered, people are often inclined against interpreting nondestructive uploading as offering a successful *transfer*. We easily recognize the unique identity of both original and upload and must then associate one or the other incompatible identities with that identity of the original subject (and from that position many people fall for the bias and prejudice described throughout this book). Similarity in either ancestry or memories is irrelevant to personhood and individuality—and for this very reason there is no such thing as *you from an alternate timeline* or someone who is *similar* to you. Similarity is off the table. Identity is binary and unyielding.

All of this reasoning can be reduced to the concise anthropic statement that you can only exist in the timeline in which you find yourself, regardless of any subsequent implications for free-will.

Conclusion

But that leaves us with the fundamental question: Do we actually have free-will or not? Does the Temporal Anthropic Principle kill free-will or is there a backdoor that can save it? As I have shown in this chapter, my preferred response is not to reject free-will at all, but rather to claim that free-will categorically makes no difference; it is causally meaningless (or perhaps more precisely, it is causally *powerless*). Anthropocism neither kills free-will nor explicitly saves it, but rather demonstrates an intrinsic categorical error in the *very question* of free-will. Time will unroll however it coincidentally unrolls. We may make free choices or we may be automatons, this question remains unanswered by temporal anthropocism, but regardless, there will only be the one true timeline, *and the one true timeline doesn't depend on free-will's truthhood*. Admittedly, the *explanation* for the timeline may depend on free-will's truthhood, but not the actual resulting events within the timeline; it will be the same timeline in either case. If the timeline is unaffected, then your mind-state sequence is unaffected, i.e., you will only occur in one way from now into the future, the way that eventually occurs.

I suspect the reason that this take on free-will has not emerged before (or has not enjoyed notable attention) is that it is significantly bolstered by my particular metaphysics, which is only newly introduced in this book. Without the metaphysics of mind-states and related sequences as a foundation, perhaps the Temporal Anthropic Principle is both more difficult to discover and to explain or defend.

Thus, free-will may or may not be true, but I conclude that it is logically pointless. As such, I consider free-will to be a red herring in philosophy of mind and am of the opinion that we should generally dismiss it from obsessive consideration.

Section 3

~ 9 ~

Interpretation of Some Scenarios

This chapter applies the theories and perspectives that I have presented to a few selections from the taxonomy. For the most part, the questions at issue are along the lines of:

1. What happened to the original mind?
2. In which brain is the original mind physically *located* following the uploading procedure?
3. Did the original mind die?
4. Did the original mind transfer (ostensibly to a different brain)?
5. Should we consider the scenario as a transfer, a copy, or a split?
6. By what analysis might we consider the procedure a successful upload?
7. By what analysis might we consider the procedure a failed attempt to upload?

§1.1.1.1
In-place destructive conscious nanobot replacement

As per the taxonomy, this procedure involves replacing individual neurons relatively independently of other neurons, either one at a time (possibly very rapidly, upwards of millions of neurons per second) or in step-wise simultaneous batches. Since the original biological brain is destroyed during this process, one of the most common challenges to mind-uploading interpretation is alleviated, namely, how to compare an uploaded brain and mind standing almost literally next to its original. However, there is still an interesting question in this scenario, namely, did the mind in question successfully survive and transfer to the computerized brain, or was it simply lost such that the subject died and a doppelganger of sorts took its place?

In general, conscious procedures lend themselves to a less contentious analysis. If there is a single continual conscious mind throughout the procedure, especially if the brain housing the mind spans a fully connected physical structure at all times, partly biological and partly computerized at various intermediate stages, then it is easier to accept the preservation of those traits generally considered crucial to identity. We could even say that the mind resulting from the upload has had essentially the same experience that it would have otherwise had if it had remained biological and never uploaded in the first place (that is to say, the subject need not even know they have been uploaded). The mind still consists of a smooth sequence of mind-states meandering through mind-state space and its continuity in both space and time has been preserved (with the caveat of the minor spatial discontinuities that are required and which sum to hundreds or thousands of kilometers, as described in §1.1.1.1).

Consequently, §1.1.1.1 generally raises the least challenge to most people when considering or contemplating mind-uploading scenarios. If one is going to accept mind-uploading at all (and not everyone will of course) then they will almost certainly accept this scenario.

§1.1.2.1
In-place nondestructive conscious nanobot brain-doubling

This scenario was a fairly strange addition to the taxonomy. I came up with it on my own and am unaware that anyone else has thought of it before. The procedure is similar to §1.1.1.1 except that instead of killing the biological neurons and attaching to their synaptic connections, the nanobots replicate a second computerized network alongside the biological network. The result is two topologically identical networks housed in the same skull, interwoven through one another, receiving identical sensory input from the same vantage point in the world, but remaining functionally and causally disconnected. Certain elements of this scenario are left unstated, such as where the upload's external motor signals go (perhaps they simply vanish, giving the upload the sensation of helplessly *riding* inside a puppet).

At first glance, it may seem simple to disregard the upload as *legitimate* since the biological brain and its mind are clearly unaffected by the procedure—but the catch is that the resulting computerized brain is, by definition of the scenario, materially identical to that which resulted from §1.1.1.1. Given two scenarios which produce the same material result, how can we logically consider one scenario to be a successful *transfer* and the other to be a qualified failure? From the POV of the upload, the scenarios are indistinguishable, so how can we judge them differently? Lest the reader argue that a distinction might be made with regard to the disconnected motor signals mentioned above, then consider a subtle variant in which the upload is *handed control* of the output signals and the biological original is the one left muscularly disconnected. Would such a challenger happily grant the identity to the upload as quickly as they raised the challenge? As I have argued, the resolution that suffers the least logical incoherence is two part: first, to permit minds to conceptually split (as opposed to necessarily *transferring* or disparagingly *copying*), and second, to regard the various minds resulting from a split as being of equal primacy to the original mind even if one of the resulting minds actually is the original mind still housed in the original brain. I admit this is a difficult proposition for many readers to accept.

§1.1.2.1.1
Brain-doubling with temporary biological shutdown

This scenario bridges a conceptual gap between §1.1.1.1 and §1.1.2.1, both of which were just presented in the previous sections. To start off, it operates similarly to §1.1.1.1, with nanobots taking over the functionality of neurons on a per-neuron basis. However, as a nanobot takes over, its assigned neuron is not killed, but rather put into a dormant state, and the nanobot connects to its synapses. Much like §1.1.1.1, neural processing steadily shifts from the biological brain to the computerized brain, all the while preserving a single fully connected brain and a single conscious mind. An important detail is that when the second nanobot of a synapse takes over, the computerized synapse is essentially disconnected from both now-dormant neurons.

In §1.1.1.1, the neurons would now be dead, but in §1.1.2.1.1 the neurons are merely dormant and no longer a functional part of the continually conscious and running brain. If the biological brain is then left indefinitely dormant (or even perhaps destroyed after the procedure), then this scenario is essentially §1.1.1.1 and the mind has simply *transferred*, in agreement with our basic intuitions. However, the dormant biological brain still has potential, unlike in §1.1.1.1. Thus, this scenario is also essentially §1.1.2.1, with a *doubled* computerized brain residing in the original skull. The only difference between §1.1.2.1. and §1.1.2.1.1 is that the biological brain is initially dormant (static) following the procedure. To exacerbate the situation, we can also consider §1.1.2.1.1.1, a minor variant in which the upload's brain resides not in the original skull, but in a completely different body. This scenario leaves the original person—both brain and body—completely unaltered, while at the same time further challenging our biases and prejudices by explicitly implying that the procedure yields two utterly disconnected people. Yet, any straightforward interpretation would clearly assign the original identity to the upload!

So what then are we to make of the possibility of reawakening the dormant biological brain? At first glance this may seem to simply invoke §1.1.2.1, with two brains along side each other in the same skull (or in the case of §1.1.2.1.1.1, bodily separated but otherwise simply doubled), but there is a crucial difference. In §1.1.2.1 there is greater contention as to whether the *original* mind *transferred* to the computerized brain or whether it was merely *copied* while leaving the original mind intact in the biological brain. In §1.1.2.1.1 and §1.1.2.1.1.1, such a conclusion is much more challenging since a conscious and fully con-nected mind (and only *one* mind at any given instant) steadily trans-ferred functionality from the biological brain to the computerized brain. As stated, one possible, yet astounding, analysis of §1.1.2.1.1 is that the original mind is truly in the computerized brain and that the reawakened biological brain now houses the duplicate mind!

Of course, the most equitable interpretation is to dispense with notions of originality and duplication entirely, and to adopt the termi-nology and perspective of splits instead. Seen this way, the scenario simply produces one descendant mind in the computerized brain, which was conscious the entire time, and a second descendant mind in the biological brain, which briefly entered a dormant state during the procedure and then awakened afterwards[26]. Both resulting minds con-sist of sequences of mind-states with a common history (ancestry) up to a point and then diverging in sequence after that point.

One thing to point out is that it was proposed above that the dor-mant biological brain could conceivably be destroyed instead of being reawakened. While this turn of events shouldn't affect our interpreta-tion of the identity of the upload, the fact that the biological brain could reawaken and offer a second mind shows that destroying it would be a form of death for a legitimate and distinct mind, a person, regardless of our notions of originality or duplication.

As a final twist, it might be argued that by destroying a mind in its sleep when it has been transferred/duplicated/split, the mind was never permitted to complete the split into a *second* mind (the two se-quences never truly diverged) and therefore that nothing (no one) has

---

[26] We shouldn't be too troubled by dormancy itself, since brains lose consciousness all the time. Not only do we lose consciousness, or at least experience a stunted and radically dissimilar form it, during admittedly neurally-active sleep, but we also readily survive situations such as fainting, anesthesia, coma, etc. However, perhaps the most spectacular example is that of a few rare cases of rapid frigid drowning—submerged for upwards of an hour mind you—in which the brain drops in temperature so quickly that the subse-quent loss of oxygen causes no long term harm. The revived patients regain their identity with no philosophical qualms. These few cases demonstrate that cryonics, even if techno-logically speculative (for no method of revival is yet available, despite numerous patients having already undergone the procedure), is nevertheless *philosophically* sound. Likewise, any dormancy associated with mind-uploading is also unproblematic.

been lost or killed. After all, such an analysis closely mirrors why we generally consider §1.1.1.1 to be acceptable and not a form of death.

§2.1.1
Frozen destructive scan-and-copy

The frozen destructive scan-and-copy procedure is worth discussing for the simple reason that it is by far the most technologically feasible scenario in the taxonomy. Aside from any metaphysical speculation, we will most likely gain the capability of performing this procedure before any others. In fact, elements of this procedure are already standard practice in neuroscience. The basic approach consists of freezing a brain (not necessarily literally, but nevertheless halting its dynamic evolution and preserving its final brain-state with minimal damage) and then slicing it into the thinnest possible two-dimensional sections. The sections are scanned as ostensible two-dimensional images (contingent on the thickness of the slices) and then the three-dimensional connectome structure is inferred and reconstructed in software.

There are several ways in which the current practice differs from how theoretical mind-uploading would operate, both in terms of methodology and intent. The current use of these kinds of procedures presumes that the subject is indisputably dead before the procedure is performed (in this way the procedure differs from similar studies into suspended animation [48]). It further differs in that there is no intent whatsoever of attempting to cognitively upload or revive the subject. Even where subsequent experiments and applications may involve running functional simulations on the resulting connectome model, there is no philosophical interpretation of such experiments that such a model represents an *upload* of any sort, but rather merely offers a view into generalized brain behavior. In short, current intent and applications are for the pure science of studying the connectome and understanding the canonical brain (not a particular brain) as a goal in and of itself. Furthermore, some (not all) current practices along these lines don't scan a single subject's brain, but rather scan numerous brains and produce a conglomerated model that represents an average (of sorts), which is clearly conceptually distinct from intending to scan and *capture* an individual brain, much less its mind. Doubtless, the scientists working hard on both applying and improving these procedures would not readily admit that there is much of a connection between their solemn work and an idea as scientifically tenuous as mind-uploading.

With that legitimate concern voiced, there are two primary challenges to extending current practice to conceivable mind-uploading. The first challenge concerns the necessary technological improvements or extensions that uploading would presumably require, for example decreasing whatever damage may occur during the slice-and-scan process, increasing the spatial resolution both in terms of slice-thickness and scan quality, and improving the quality of connectome inference from the scanned sections.

The second challenge is more serious. It remains to be seen to what extent the connectome alone (the network topology) embeds neural function sufficient to produce a mind. A cognitive algorithm which operates (or can be inferred) purely as a function of network topology should be quite amenable to a frozen scan-and-copy approach (a simple example might be retinal receptive fields, the basic operation of which is relatively simple to understand merely from the way in which retinal cells are interconnected). On the other hand, it is quite possible that many higher-order cognitive algorithms performed in the brain rely not exclusively on network topology but also on intra-cellular state, regional chemical environments, action potential *spike-timing synchronization*, electrical brain-wave phenomena, or other unstated functional aspects of the brain that are not easily discerned from mere static structure. Some of these properties might be deducible from futuristic static scans as well, while some may not. If certain aspects of neural function are positively required by uploading but cannot be ascertained from a frozen scan, then all bets are off for frozen scan methods and such procedures will have to be replaced (or at least combined) with on-line live functional scans of some sort.

Aside from the genuine challenges posed to the feasibility of the procedure itself, the hypothetical metaphysical analysis is unaffected. Assuming the procedure is justified on physical grounds, we can consider the status of the resulting mind. On one hand, this procedure is quite similar to §1.1.1.1. The biological brain is destroyed and an artificial brain (either computerized or virtual) is produced. The reason most people are less comfortable with this scenario is two-fold: one, that it does not occur during consciousness and thereby does not preserve a continually conscious mind as it transfers from the biological brain to the artificial brain, and two, that it involves a macroscopic spatial discontinuity with the new brain residing at a definitively different location from the biological brain.

One could argue that many of our medical procedures operate on a similar assumption that preserving consciousness is unimportant, i.e., that a loss of consciousness is irrelevant to the identity of the mind that awakens after surgery. Of course, no existing surgery involves whole-parcel replacement of the brain's substrate while claiming to preserve the associated mind. It is up to the reader to decide his or her own philosophical stance on that issue. Furthermore, the process is entirely consistent with this book's metaphysics, namely that a smooth sequence of mind-states yields a single and identifiable mind, regardless of substrate transitions or temporary unconsciousness along the way.

On the second point, that of large spatial discontinuity, recall that the spatial continuity classically presumed in the case of §1.1.1.1 actually fails under closer scrutiny (as presented in that section of the taxonomy) so we must contend with some degree of spatial discontinuity anyway. In addition to that point, the metaphysics that has been presented is entirely tolerant of spatial discontinuities. A mind, conceived of as a sequence of mind-states, has absolutely no reliance on spatial continuity whatsoever. In fact, a mind is a definitively nonspatial metaphysical entity. Another way to look at this issue was illustrated in an earlier section where it was demonstrated that our perception of spatial discontinuity is easily interrupted using modern technologies like televisions and computer displays which can present arbitrary visual stimuli to a subject, thereby giving the illusion of rampant spatial discontinuity (teleportation) without the slightest harm to our sense of self, identity, or personhood. Consequently, speaking only for myself, I am utterly unconvinced by arguments that there should be any special status to spatial continuity whatsoever.

§2.1.2.1
Frozen nondestructive scan-and-copy:
Natural environments

Both brains are awakened in naturally
varying sensory environments

The next three scenarios are all closely related in the taxonomy. They present three variations on a frozen nondestructive scan-and-copy procedure. The premise is the same in all three cases: the subject's original biological brain is first put into a static but nondestructive and unharmful state (perhaps cryonic preservation as one example). The brain is then somehow nondestructively scanned, an admittedly challenging concept even in hypothetical terms but nevertheless permissible for the riveting philosophical questions it raises. The scan is then copied and instantiated in an artificial brain, either computerized or virtual. At this point, we can consider various scenarios in which the two unconscious brains might be reawakened to resume consciousness.

Lest it not yet be clear at this point, the metaphysics that has been presented obviates any question as to whether the two minds, the two people, should be considered one and the same. The instant they regain consciousness, their mind-state sequences (aka, their minds) split along different paths through mind-state space, and consequently establish full autonomy from one another—with the possible exception explored below with respect to §2.1.2.3.

First, let us consider §2.1.2.1, in which the two minds awaken in reasonable varying environments, say on two different surgical operating tables. This is the easiest scenario to analyze in terms of identity since they clearly differ in their experiences. The fundamental question that remains, however, is how we should assign primacy to the resulting minds; who gets to consider themselves the *true* mind and who should be relegated to secondary status? Many people would favor the brain and mind of the original biological brain, especially in light of the realization that the original person need not even be aware that an upload process has occurred. Surely, if they are the same person as if an upload had not occurred, despite temporarily being put into stasis, then they should be regarded as the original even if an upload did occur. However, as has been presented, there is another interpretation. Two sequences of mind-states now exist. They have a common ancestry, by which I mean their sequences are identical up to a point in time, and then they diverge from that time onward. There is no particular reason, in my opinion, to assign greater ownership of the original identity to either of the two minds in question. The metaphysics of brains and minds cares not a whit as to which particular atoms make up any given brain and whether those same atoms were present in the original brain prior to the uploading procedure.

This analysis raises the question however, should the mind-uploading process be characterized as a success or a failure? People argue about this issue with impressive commitment. I would propose that the question is simply ill-formed. It is posed as if there must be only one answer, either success or failure, but I prefer the interpretation that there is potentially a distinct and valid answer for each subjective perspective that we could query. From one mind's (one person's) perspective, the process has failed, and from another mind's it has succeeded. To those readers who would leap upon this statement as a concession that the process has failed, I would reiterate that in my analysis no superiority can be granted to the perspective, values, or feelings of either of the two minds. Consequently, I would rather insistently state that the process has both failed and succeeded to equal degrees. I would no more concede the procedure's failure than I would insist upon its success. This is, admittedly, a pretty difficult philosophical position to hold as it requires straddling a seemingly unstable interpretation, in which the slightest momentary inclination gravitates toward one of the extreme conclusions of favoring one mind's POV over the other, but I urge the reader to attempt to hold in his or her mind the notion that both conclusions can be equally true at the same time.

§2.1.2.2
Frozen nondestructive scan-and-copy:
Identical environments

Both brains are awakened in essentially
identical sensory environments

This scenario differs from the previous scenario in that the two minds awaken in environments that, as far as external stimuli are concerned, are causally and experientially identical. The simplest way to conceive of such a scenario is to imagine a minimal environment, say a completely empty windowless room. Given that physical determinism may very well be false (as discussed earlier), the two minds would instantly, if imperceptibly, split in their mind-state sequences and thereby gain instant uniqueness of identity and personhood. That is why this scenario is discussed here, to emphasize that there is no need to debate whether the two resulting minds are *the same person* or some such interpretation. They are distinct the moment they gain consciousness for the metaphysical reason that their mind-state sequences instantly diverge to unique mind-states and thereafter never again merge.

All the same questions pertaining to primacy of the original identity could be considered, but such questions are equally answered in the previous section analyzing §2.1.2.1. Rather, let's simply consider the question of how quickly we would expect the behavior and/or internal mental experiences of the two people in question to diverge. How long would it take for macroscopic changes in motor behavior to surface, say the raising of a finger by one person, but not the other, or the glancing to the left by one, but not the other. How long would it take for the two people in question to appear to an outsider as entirely uncorrelated in their respective lives? Furthermore, at what rate could we describe their internal mental states as diverging to varying degrees (and how would we quantify such differences in mind-state?)?

§2.1.2.3
Frozen nondestructive scan-and-copy:
The White Room

Both brains are awakened in identical
sensory environments in a deterministic universe

The White Room, as I call it, is a fascinating thought experiment, even if physically implausible. In a deterministic universe (and therefore quite possibly not our own universe) we can consider awakening the two minds in identical environments and observing both their external behavior and their internal mental states. By definition of the scenario, both these sets of observations would match. External behavior would operate in lock-step synchronization forever, literally for years. Fifty years after the uploading procedure, when one person lifts his left arm and rotates it clockwise at the wrist, the other will perform the exact same action at the same time. Likewise, all internal mental states would agree. Every thought, feeling, and cogitation would occur in absolute synchrony between the two minds.

The metaphysical interpretation is that the single original mind, which represented a sequence of mind-states, a path through mind-state space, became doubled in a second brain-state token, such that two brains-states embedded the same mind-state. So far, this is not a remarkable statement and would accurately reflect other scenarios as well. What makes this scenario so incredible is that the two brains (sequences of brain-states) then meandered through brain-state space (and corresponding mind-state space) along parallel paths after the upload procedure. In what sense did they *split*? They are certainly *doubled*, but have they meaningfully split? Are they unique? Are they two entities, or a single entity? At the token level, they are two, but at the type level, they refer to the same type—which cannot exist multiple times, so should we conclude that they actually refer to a single mind, a single person in effect?

§2.2.1.1
Conscious destructive scan-and-copy: Teleportation

This scenario is worth discussing a little bit since it is tantamount to teleportation and often crops up in debates over mind-uploading metaphysics. Frankly, I don't think there is too much to add, and the reader should, at this point, be able to interpret the scenario according to the metaphysics this book presents. Given that I see no rationale in honoring spatial continuity, and given that the sequence of mind-states representing the mind in question is smooth and relatively continuous, it should be clear that this scenario (and any related notion of teleportation) is entirely compatible with the offered metaphysics. This scenario gets more interesting when extrapolated to the next scenario, which involves a nondestructive scan.

§2.2.2.1
Conscious nondestructive scan-and-copy

This scenario is essentially teleportation in which the scanning step is not definitively destructive, but rather requires an after-the-fact destruction step to complete the teleportation, or the upload process as the case may be. There is, of course, a crucial problem with this scenario, one which is entirely accommodated by this book's metaphysics. If the subject is conscious throughout the procedure, and if the scan is nondestructive, then there can be absolutely no doubt that the mind splits into two distinct minds consisting of two partially unique sequences of mind-states. As such, both the personhood and the uniqueness of both minds is beyond dispute and consequently any prescribed after-the-fact destruction step is a simple killing, no less. This conclusion has no bearing on whether we judge the teleportation or upload process as a success or failure. The reader should understand at this point that the interpretation I offer is that of simultaneous success and failure, both to equal degrees. I won't belabor that point here again. The only point worth making is that since this procedure clearly involves killing a singular, autonomous, and unique person, it is absurd and shouldn't be given serious consideration in mind-uploading or teleportation metaphysical debates, even though it keeps coming up for philosophically unrefined reasons.

§3. Brain division

The third major category of the taxonomy, brain division, (after in-place replacement and scan-and-copy procedures) offers rich opportunities for analysis. I like the brain division scenarios because they can seemingly undermine certain conclusions often drawn from the other scenarios. For simplicity, let us assume that the original brain is static and its mind is unconscious during the procedure. After division and rebuilding of the resulting brains, they are then awakened and their respective status considered.

The first scenario is a 50% division. The two resulting brains are half biological and half computerized. Clearly we cannot reasonably grant one greater primacy than the other with respect to the original mind. Bear in mind that considerations of left/right hemisphere heterogeneity are irrelevant since the division need not be sagittal, regional, spatially bipartite (two non-interwoven portions), or even macroscopic (see figure 3, subfigure B). In my view, the metaphysics are relatively straightforward. The original brain (a sequence of brain-states embedded in a brain-state token in temporal flux, albeit frozen for the duration of the procedure) became doubled as two instantiated frozen brain-state tokens (neither more original than the other, of course). When consciousness resumed, the two brains then immediately split in their respective paths through brain-state space—and their associated minds split in a corresponding manner. This interpretation aligns nicely with several of the other scenarios that have been presented so far.

The question of where the original mind went is both seemingly more challenging, and yet at the same time, ultimately more easily resolved than in other scenarios. It seems more challenging since we can't easily point to where the one original mind *went* (in so far as a mind has a spatial location at all), and yet since there are clearly two resulting minds, we know *the* mind somehow survived, regardless of whether it is difficult to explain. The resolution to this dilemma is actually easier than in other scenarios because we don't have to decide how to delegate the original mind's identity between the two resulting minds; the perfect equivalence of the two brains and minds in this scenario utterly obviates the asymmetries that plague and confuse our interpretation of other scenarios. In fact, the 50% division scenario illustrates the preeminent theory of *mind splitting* more perfectly and unambiguously than any other scenario presented in the taxonomy. Surely, if any scenario illustrates the concept of mind splitting with unassailable clarity, it is the 50% division scenario.

The other division scenarios present additional challenges. What about the 1% / 99% division? Should we consider either resulting brain as housing *the* original to the detriment of the other brain? While various readers may arrive at a range of conclusions on this scenario, the metaphysics presented offers the following interpretation. Given a complete disregard for notions of spatial or material continuity, and given that minds are defined purely as nonspatial sequences of mind-states, we would conclude that both brains and both minds may make equal claim to the original identity—which has obviously split just as in other scenarios. The fact that one of the two brains is 99% original biological substrate is irrelevant to such an analysis.

We then come to the 1/100-billionth division, in which one of the two brains consists of the original biological brain but with the replacement of a single neuron with a corresponding nanobot while the other brain contains a single biological neuron from the original brain and with the rest of the brain computerized. This scenario is, of course, identical to the very first step in a gradual in-place replacement scenario (§1.1.1) from the point of view of the mostly biological brain. However, it offers a secondary analysis, that pertaining to the second brain containing but a single neuron. The metaphysics presented suggests that we can rightly permit both brains equal primacy to the original identity! I accept that many readers will reject such an interpretation, but this is the metaphysics I have established and which best serves my own philosophy.

Other brain division scenarios suggest the possibility of producing multiple uploads at once. The 33% scenario proposes a method by which three brains and minds could result, each containing an equal portion of the original brain. The 1% scenario proposes creating 100 such brains, and the ultimate scenario of this type theorizes the creation of *100 billion resulting brains*, each no more (and crucially, no less) original than the others! The analysis in these cases is essentially identical to the 50% scenario. Rather astoundingly, we can conclude that not only is an upload equal to the original in primacy of identity, but that a near incomprehensible number of such uploads may all come into existence and achieve equal status in one fell swoop.

∼ **10** ∼

Conclusion

This book was presented in three major sections. The first section, following the introduction, consists of chapters two and three, a glossary and taxonomy. Chapter two established a glossary of terms relevant to discussions of mind-uploading so that the rest of the book would have a foundation from which to proceed. Chapter three presented a taxonomy of mind-uploading scenarios and thought experiments. Some of the scenarios offered are common in the mind-uploading canon while others are virtually brand new, having been conceived of and added by me during the development of the taxonomy. Chapters four through eight represented the second section, in which I presented one possible metaphysical philosophy of mind that I believe is fairly consistent and enables logical and reasoned analysis of what minds are and what sorts of transformations we should expect minds to be capable of undergoing. The third section, chapter nine, offered a brief survey of a few scenarios from the taxonomy, interpreted through the lens of the established metaphysics.

I have multiple goals for this book. For those readers who are not persuaded by the metaphysical presentation, I still hope they find the glossary, and to a greater extent, the taxonomy, helpful in developing their own philosophy of mind and mind-uploading. However, I hope that the metaphysical presentation has succeeded in convincing at least some readers of its underlying validity. Multiple propositions have been offered, any of which may find purchase with various readers.

First, I have provided a metaphysical theory of what minds and mind-states actually are, and how they relate to brains and brain-states. I have also described the basic transformations that should be possible on brains and minds, conceived as minimal *epsilon* differences between temporally adjacent state pairs. I have also described those transformations which should explicitly *not* be possible, namely merging minds forward in time, which is tantamount to permitting a single mind-state to arise from multiple prior possible mind-states.

Second, I have attempted to present and argue for the concept that minds can readily *split*, that they can do so practically on a whim in various mind-uploading scenarios.

Third, I have proposed that following such a split, the primacy of the resulting minds is equal across a wide spectrum of uploading scenarios, even if one of the resulting minds is still associated with the original brain. Where supporting such an equality of primacy to the original mind would seemingly raise a paradox (how can two undeniably distinct people both equally correctly claim to be the same original person?) I have explained that multiple equally valid subjective perspectives are entitled to their own potentially conflicting interpretations of the circumstances and that no perspective can easily be favored without resorting to bias or prejudice.

Fourth and ultimately, I hope to put a dent in the risk of bias, prejudice, and eventual discrimination that could easily result from alternative philosophical stances on these issues.

To reiterate an earlier point, the hypothetical circumstances presented are not too serious yet since they are not remotely feasible, so we can enjoy the simple recreation that this philosophical musing currently offers—but someday these or related technologies may become more plausible, and we might benefit from evaluating such biases as early as possible.

~ ~ ~

Thank you for reading this book. If you enjoyed it, please consider leaving a review at your favorite retailer.

—Keith Wiley

Bibliography

1. Amunts K., Lepage C., Borgeat L., Mohlberg H., Dickscheid T., Rousseau M., Bludau S., Bazin P., Lewis L. B., Oros-Peusquens A., Shah N. J., Lippert T., Zilles K., Evans A. C. BigBrain: An Ultrahigh-Resolution 3D Human Brain Model. *Science*. vol. 340(6139), pp. 1472–1475, 2013.

2. BBC. 1997, last accessed on 2014-06-01. Available at: http://www.arkive.org/african-river-martin/pseudochelidon-eurystomina/video-06.html.

3. Beebe W. *Edge of the Jungle*. Henry Holt and Company. pp. 291–294, 1921.

4. Bickle J. Multiple Realizability. 2013, last accessed on 2014-06-07. Available at: http://plato.stanford.edu/entries/multiple-realizability/.

5. Borges J. L. *Collected Fictions*. The Garden of Forking Paths (1941), The Library of Babel. Allen Lane, The Penguin Press. 1999.

6. Brown J. Playmate Meets Geeks Who Made Her a Net Star. *Wired*. vol. 5, 1997.

7. Chalmers D. Facing up to the problem of consciousness. *Journal of Consciousness Studies*. vol. 2(3), pp. 200–219, 1995.

8. Chalmers D. *The Conscious Mind*. Oxford University Press. 1996.

9. Cleve F. M. *Philosophy of Anaxagoras*. King's Crown Press, Columbia University, New York. 1949.

10. Crockford D. The JSON Saga. 2009, last accessed on 2014-07-26. Available at: https://www.youtube.com/watch?v=-C-JoyNuQJs.

11. Dawkins R. *River Out of Eden*. BasicBooks, HarperCollins. pp. 66–67, 1995.

12. Dennett D. *Elbow Room: The Varieties of Free Will Worth Wanting*. MIT Press. 1984.

13. Dennett D. *Consciousness Explained*. Little, Brown and Company. 1991.

14. Dennett D. *Darwin's Dangerous Idea*. Simon & Schuster, New York. 1995.

15. Eddington A. S. *Nature of the Physical World*. The Macmillan Company, New York & The University Press, Cambridge. 1927.

16. Frege G. *The Foundations of Arithmetic*. 2nd revised edition. Harper & Brothers. 1953.

17. Hameroff S., Penrose R. Consciousness in the universe: A review of the 'Orch OR' theory. *Physics of Life Reviews*. vol. 11(1), pp. 39–78, 2014.

18. Hamming R. W. Error Detecting and Error Correcting Codes. *Bell System Technical Journal*. vol. 29, pp. 147–160, 1950.

19. Hampson R. E., Song D., Opris I., Santos L. M., Shin D. C., Gerhardt G. A., Marmarelis V. Z., Berger T. W., Deadwyler S. A. Facilitation of memory encoding in primate hippocampus by a neuroprosthesis that promotes task-specific neural firing. *Journal of Neural Engineering*. vol. 10(6), pp. 066013+, December 2013.

20. Hayworth K. Killed by Bad Philosophy. 2010, last accessed on 2014-08-04. Available at: http://brainpreservation.org/content/killed-bad-philosophy.

21. Hoefer C. Causal Determinism. 2010, last accessed on 2014-05-26. Available at: http://plato.stanford.edu/archives/spr2010/entries/determinism-causal/.

22. Hölldobler B., Wilson E. O. *The Ants*. The Belknap Press of Harvard University Press. pp. 585–586, 1990.

23. Kolomogorov A. N. On tables of random numbers. *Sankhyā*. vol. 25(4), pp. 369–376, 1963.

24. Kolomogorov A. N. Three approaches to the quantitative definition of information. *International Journal of Computer Mathematics*. 1968.

25. Kurzweil R. *The Age of Spiritual Machines: When Computers Exceed Human Intelligence*. Viking, New York. 1999.

26. Kurzweil R. *The Singularity is Near: When Humans Transcend Biology*. Viking, New York. 2005.

27. Landauer R. Irreversibility and Heat Generation in the Computing Process. *IBM J. Res. Dev.* vol. 5(3), pp. 183–191, July 1961.

28. Lodish H., Berk A., Zipursky S. L., Matsudaira P., Baltimore D., Darnell J. *Molecular Cell Biology*. ch. 21.2 The Action Potential and Conduction of Electric Impulses. W. H. Freeman, New York. 2000.

29. McLaughlin B., Bennett K. Supervenience. 2011, last accessed on 2014-06-06. Available at: http://plato.stanford.edu/entries/supervenience/.

30. Minsky M. *The Society of Mind*. Simon & Schuster, New York. 1985.

31. Moravec H. *Mind Children: The Future of Robot and Human Intelligence*. Harvard University Press, Cambridge. 1988.

32. Moravec H. *Robot: Mere Machine to Transcendent Mind*. Oxford University Press, New York. 1999.

33. Nietzsche F. *Thus Spoke Zarathustra*. Ernst Schmeitzner. 1883.

34. Nietzsche F. *Beyond Good and Evil*. 1886.

35. Oh S. W., Harris J. A., Ng L., Winslow B., Cain N., Mihalas S., Wang Q., Lau C., Kuan L., Henry A. M., Mortrud M. T., Ouellette B., Nguyen T. N., Sorensen S. A., Slaughterbeck C. R., Wakeman W., Li Y., Feng D., Ho A., Nicholas E., Hirokawa K. E., Bohn P., Joines K. M., Peng H., Hawrylycz M. J., Phillips J. W., Hohmann J. G., Wohnoutka P., Gerfen C. R., Koch C., Bernard A., Dang C., Jones A. R., Zeng H. A mesoscale connectome of the mouse brain. *Nature*. 2014.

36. Paul G., Cox E. *Beyond Humanity: Cyberevolution and Future Minds*. Delmar Thomson Learning. 1996.

37. Sadi Z. Katydid video. 2014, last accessed on 2014-05-26. Available at: https://www.youtube.com/watch?v=ZbIHK28Zl0M.

38. Sartre J. *Existentialism and Human Emotions*. Citadel Press, Kensington Pub. Corp.. 1957.

39. Schneirla T. *Army Ants: A Study in Social Organization*. W. H. Freeman & Co Ltd. 1971.

40. Searle J. R. *Minds, Brains and Science*. Harvard University Press, Cambridge. 1984.

41. Searle J. R. *The Mystery of Consciousness*. The New York Review of Books. 1997.

42. Searle J. R. Why I Am Not a Property Dualist. *Journal of Consciousness Studies*. 2002.

43. Seife C. *Decoding the Universe: How the New Science of Information Is Explaining Everything in the Cosmos, from Our Brains to Black Holes*. Viking, New York. 2006.

44. Shannon C. A Mathematical Theory of Communication. *Bell System Technical Journal*. vol. 27, pp. 379–423, 623–656, July, October 1948.

45. Stein G. *Geography and Plays*. ch. Sacred Emily. Four Seas, Boston. 1922.

46. Stroud J. M. The fine structure of psychological time. *Information theory in psychology*. pp. 174–205, 1956.

47. Superman Logo. 2014, last accessed on 2014-06-07. Available at: http://en.wikipedia.org/wiki/Superman_logo.

48. Thomson H. Gunshot victims to be suspended between life and death. *NewScientist*. vol. 2962, Mar. 2014.

49. Wetzel L. Types and Tokens. 2014, last accessed on 2014-05-26. Available at: http://plato.stanford.edu/archives/spr2014/entries/types-tokens/.

50. Wiley K. Gnat Cloud. 1999, last accessed on 2014-05-26. Available at: http://keithwiley.com/artificialLife/gnatCloud.shtml.

51. Wiley K. Implications of Computerized Intelligence on Interstellar Travel. *H+ Magazine*. 2011.

52. Wiley K. The Fermi Paradox, Self-Replicating Probes, and the Interstellar Transportation Bandwidth. *arXiv:1111.6131*. 2011.

53. Wiley K. Response to Susan Schneider's The Philosophy of 'Her'. *H+ Magazine*. 2014.

54. Wiley R. H. *Noise Matters: Evolution of Communication in Noise*. Harvard University Press, Cambridge. Forthcoming 2015.

Index

3D printer 77
3D scanner 77

Ambiguity 15, 81-82, 85, 88
ant 114, 117-118
ant mill 117-118
ant, army 117
anthropicism 135-143
antimatter 77
archeology 83
Aristotle 28-29, 69-70, 100
artifact 6, 82-83, 87
artificial intelligence 19, 86
atom 79, 86, 89-90, 104-105, 131-132, 156
awake 16, 21, 55, 92-93

Bandwidth 40-41
basket star 49
bias 4, 24, 65-67, 142, 150, 164
binary 76, 100-101, 142
bit string 26, 76-79, 89, 92, 110
Boltzmann 76
Borges, Jorge Luis 101
brain 4-9, 11, 17-25, 29, 32-39, 42-48, 50-61, 66-68, 76-78, 82-99, 101, 104, 109-113, 116, 121-127, 129-133, 147-158, 160-162, 164
brain division 34, 57, 60-61, 160-161
brain scan 86, 90
brain-doubling 33, 41, 43-44, 46-48, 148-149

brain-in-a-vat 77-78
brain-state 20, 29, 95-99, 101, 104-108, 129, 132, 152, 158, 160
brain-state space 101, 104, 107, 129, 158
brittle star 49
bush-robot 33, 47-48

Carbon 79, 86
Cartesian theater 124
Chalmers, David 27, 69, 112, 115, 121-122, 124-126, 128
chess 90-91
clone 24, 45, 51, 57-59, 67, 93, 141
communication 9, 121
conceptualism 69
connectome 50, 152-153
consciousness 6-7, 11, 16-17, 21-22, 33-36, 41-48, 50-52, 55-57, 69, 77, 86, 92-93, 96, 102, 109-111, 114-117, 119-130, 133, 137-138, 147-148, 150-151, 154-155, 157, 159-160
continuity, spatial 25, 33, 37, 40-43, 47-48, 154-155, 159
continuity, temporal 21, 36, 42
copy 24, 67, 86, 90, 109-111, 127, 147, 149-150, 155
cortical column 20, 29, 32, 52
Crick 121
cricket 117, 119
Crockford, Douglas 70
cryogenics 22
cryonics 22, 151, 155

crystal 77, 79, 81, 86
culture 65, 82-83, 85, 87-88

Debate 4-5, 10-11, 13-15, 21, 46, 55, 67-
   68, 92, 111-113, 115, 121, 126, 128, 138,
   157, 159-160
Dennett, Daniel 27, 69, 77-78, 101, 124,
   126-128
Descartes 111
destructive 33-34, 36, 41-44, 46-48, 50, 54-
   57, 103, 138, 142, 147-148, 152, 155, 157-
   159
determinism 26, 34, 54, 92-93, 135-137,
   140, 157-158
diamond 79
digit 28, 47, 73-76, 82, 85-86, 96
discrimination 66, 164
dualism 11, 89-91, 110-114, 123-124
dualism, Cartesian 111
dualism, naturalistic 112
dualism, property 112-113, 122
duplicate 6-7, 24, 43-45, 48, 51, 55, 67, 77,
   109-110, 115, 151
dynamic 7-8, 15-16, 21, 23, 26-27, 36, 42,
   47, 50, 55, 90-92, 95-97, 122-123, 129-
   130, 152

Einstein 76-77
emergence 8-9, 110, 112-113, 122, 124, 126-
   127
energy 5, 76-77, 104
entropy 26, 76-77
equality 58, 60, 66-67, 76, 110, 130-132,
   149, 156, 159, 161-162, 164
existentialism 11, 138-140

Five 11, 20, 41-42, 53-54, 73-74, 78-79, 81-
   85, 89-90, 101, 110, 147
flight 78, 95, 122-123
flight simulator 78
flock 8, 114, 118, 122-125

Fourier analysis 96
free-will 11, 26, 94, 107, 110, 133, 135-140,
   142-143
freedom 26, 138-140
frozen 21-22, 33, 42-43, 46-47, 50, 54, 56-
   57, 86, 90-92, 94-95, 97-98, 152-153, 155,
   157-158, 160

Gnat Cloud 118
Gorgonocephalus eucnemis 49
gradualism 21, 33, 35-36, 38-39, 42-43, 45,
   47-48, 51, 58-59, 161

Hamming distance 104
Hayworth, Kenneth 102
Heraclitus 97
homograph 81

Image-processing 71
information 20, 24, 26, 51, 54, 73, 76-77,
   79, 81-83, 85, 87, 90, 94, 101, 110, 123

JSON 70

Katydid 117, 119-120
Koch 121
Kolmogorov 26, 76, 79

Language 67, 74, 123, 132
latency 40
leetspeak 81
Lena 71
Library of Anaxagoras 101-103, 106, 112
Library of Babel 101, 104
Library of Mendel 101, 104

Matter 7, 15-16, 26, 38, 43, 55, 57, 72, 76-
   77, 79, 89-90, 94-95, 106, 112, 116, 120,
   122-123, 130, 140

metaphysics 3-4, 6, 9, 11, 15, 20, 27-29, 65, 68, 71, 78, 84-85, 88-90, 93, 96-100, 103, 110, 114, 123-125, 130-131, 135, 137, 140-141, 143, 152-161, 163-164

mind 3-9, 11, 13, 15-17, 19-26, 29, 32, 35, 39-40, 44-47, 51-52, 54-59, 61, 65-69, 71, 76-78, 82-90, 92-94, 96-103, 106, 108-113, 115-117, 122-123, 125, 128-133, 135, 137-138, 140-143, 147-151, 153-164

mind-state 15, 86, 96-98, 101-103, 105-109, 129, 132, 137, 142-143, 148, 155, 157-158, 164

mind-state space 101-103, 107-108, 129, 137, 142, 148, 155, 158

mind-uploading 3-6, 9-10, 13, 15, 23-25, 35-37, 45, 50-51, 56, 59, 65, 68, 86, 100-101, 103, 115-116, 128, 135, 141, 148, 151-153, 159, 163-164

Moravec, Hans 47

multiple realizability 85-86

Nanobot 5, 17-18, 22, 33, 36-37, 39-46, 48, 58-59, 147-148, 150, 161

network 18-19, 50-53, 124, 127, 149, 153

neuron 6-8, 17-22, 32-33, 35-48, 50, 52-53, 58-60, 96, 102, 104-105, 108, 112, 121-123, 125, 127, 147-148, 150, 153, 161

neuron-batch 33, 39, 58

Nietzsche, Friedrich 139-140

number 28, 32, 39, 57, 71, 73-74, 76, 79, 87, 91, 94, 104-105, 115, 117, 122, 162

numeral 28, 73-76, 82-83, 85-86, 96, 100-101, 110

numerical base 73

Nyquist rate 96

Occurrence 27-28, 71-73, 78-79, 89, 94, 96-101, 129

Overhuman 139

Panpsychism 113, 125

particular 10, 13, 16, 27, 31, 39, 68-69, 71, 75, 84, 86-87, 90, 100-101, 108, 110, 115, 121, 127-128, 132, 137, 141, 143, 152, 156

pattern identity theory 90-92, 113-114

physical biological 51

physical computerized 33, 51

physicalism 112-113, 126

Plato 28-29, 69-70, 83, 94, 100, 111-112

Playboy 71

point-of-view 17, 54, 56-57, 65-66, 126, 130, 132, 149, 156

polygon 69

Prefix Proposal 75

prejudice 66, 131, 142, 150, 164

primacy 11, 58, 61, 66, 109, 130-132, 138, 149, 155, 157, 160-162, 164

Qualia 115, 120, 126

quantum mechanics 18-19, 92, 136

Realism 27-29, 68-69, 94, 100

receiver 40, 77, 121

receptive field 20, 32, 52, 153

replacement rate 35, 37, 39, 42, 44

replacement, gradual 21, 33, 35, 47-48, 51

replacement, in-place 35, 43, 50, 58, 160-161

resolution, spatial 15, 21, 26-29, 33, 36, 38, 42, 50, 56-57, 86-87, 91, 94, 96-98, 103, 110, 135-143, 149, 153, 160

reversible computing 76

rose 69, 71-73, 75, 81

S 33, 81-82, 85

Sacred Emily 71

Sartre, Jean-Paul 138-140

scan-and-copy 21, 33-34, 46, 50, 54-57, 130, 152-153, 155, 157-160

scan-and-duplicate 22, 33, 35, 50

Searle, John 113, 122, 126-128

sentence 28, 69, 71-73, 75, 79, 81, 101, 124, 140

sequence 15, 20, 28-29, 73, 75-76, 81, 88-89, 95-99, 101, 103-104, 106, 108-110, 117, 129, 132, 137-138, 143, 148, 151, 154-161

Shannon, Claude 26, 73, 76

signaler 77

skull 22, 35-36, 38, 43, 45, 47-48, 58, 149-150

sleep 16-17, 56-57, 151

solipsism 120

spatio-temporal 15, 27-29, 69, 71-73, 78-79, 91, 94, 97-100, 132

spike-timing synchronization 153

split 59, 61, 94, 100-101, 103, 107-111, 129-132, 147, 149, 151, 155, 157-161, 164

starfish 49

static 15, 17, 22, 26, 42, 44, 46, 50-51, 55, 91-92, 94-97, 150, 153, 155, 160

Stein, Gertrude 71

subjective perspective 23, 58, 65, 131, 133, 156

substrate 17, 19-20, 22-23, 45, 53, 58, 127, 154, 161

substrate-independent minds 24

Superman 81, 139

supervenience 84-88

symbol 31, 81-82, 85, 87

synapse 19, 32, 43, 108, 150

system identification 7, 24

Taxonomy 4, 10-11, 23, 31-32, 41, 46-48, 50, 53, 56-57, 65, 110, 116, 128, 133, 147-148, 152, 154-155, 160-161, 163

teleportation 25, 34, 55-56, 142, 154, 159

Temporal Anthropic Principle 135-139, 141-143

The Uploading Question 16, 65, 88, 115, 128, 135

The White Room 34, 54, 91-92, 94, 158

timeline, alternate 138, 141-142

token 27-29, 68, 71-75, 78-79, 81-90, 93-94, 96-101, 109-110, 113, 129, 132, 158, 160

topology 18, 51-53, 153

transfer 4-5, 22-23, 25, 35, 37, 44-45, 47, 67, 104, 111, 115-116, 138, 142, 147-151, 154

translation 25, 33, 45-48

trope 28

type 9, 15, 20, 27-29, 35, 49, 53, 55, 68-75, 78-79, 81-88, 90, 92-94, 96-101, 103-104, 109-110, 112-113, 129, 131-133, 158, 162

Universal 27-29, 68-69, 71, 78-79, 91, 100

universe, parallel 138

Virtual functional 19, 33, 52-53

virtual higher-order 20, 33, 52

virtual reality 77

virtual structural 19, 33, 50-51

vocabulary 9, 113

Wasp, digger 116

whole brain emulation 23-24

Wiley, R 82, 120-121

Zombie 110, 114, 122, 126-128

61459946R00105

Made in the USA
Charleston, SC
21 September 2016